# The Observer's Book of
# LONDON

GEOFFREY PALMER
AND
NOEL LLOYD

WITH 15 COLOUR AND 83
BLACK AND WHITE PHOTOGRAPHS

LINE DRAWINGS BY
ROGER HARRIS

FREDERICK WARNE & CO LTD

FREDERICK WARNE & CO INC

LONDON: NEW YORK

# ACKNOWLEDGEMENTS

Thanks are given to the following copyright owners and photographers
for their kind permission to reproduce photographs in this book:

The London Museum for page 21; Colin Twinn for pages 23 (both),
131 (upper), 171 (upper), 172 (upper); A. F. Kersting for Plate 1 (both),
Plate 2 (lower), Plate 4 (both), Plate 7 (upper), Plate 8, pages 29, 30, 38
(both), 43, 45 (lower), 47, 49 (lower), 55, 59 (upper), 62, 67 (upper), 70,
75 (lower), 81 (both), 93 (upper), 95, 103, 106 (upper), 109 (lower), 113,
114, 117 (both), 121, 126, 131 (lower), 135 (upper), 147 (both), 149, 151,
152, 157 (lower), 159 (both), 161, 163, 164 (upper), 175 (lower), 178,
181 (both); Noel Lloyd for pages 33, 51, 75 (upper), 87 (lower), 155
(lower), 157 (upper), 161, 175 (upper); British Tourist Authority by
courtesy of the Dean and Chapter of Westminster, Plate 2 (upper);
British Tourist Authority for Plate 3 (both), Plate 5 (both), Plate 6 (both),
Plate 7 (lower), pages 45 (upper), 49 (upper), 59 (lower), 64, 67 (lower),
87 (upper), 93 (lower), 99, 101 (both), 104, 106 (lower), 109 (upper), 111,
135 (lower), 143 (both), 155 (upper), 164 (lower), 167 (upper), 169,
171 (lower), 172 (lower), 183; Stephen Donohoe for pages 91 and 167
(lower).

LIBRARY OF CONGRESS CATALOG
CARD NO. 73-75025

ISBN 0 7232 1515 4

*Printed in Great Britain by
William Clowes & Sons, Limited
London, Beccles and Colchester*
1248.373

*The Observer's Pocket Series*

LONDON

# The Observer Books

### A POCKET REFERENCE SERIES COVERING A
### WIDE RANGE OF SUBJECTS

*Natural History*
BIRDS
BIRDS' EGGS
BUTTERFLIES
LARGER MOTHS
COMMON INSECTS
WILD ANIMALS
ZOO ANIMALS
WILD FLOWERS
GARDEN FLOWERS
FLOWERING TREES
          AND SHRUBS
HOUSE PLANTS
CACTI
TREES
GRASSES
FERNS
COMMON FUNGI
LICHENS
POND LIFE
FRESHWATER FISHES
SEA FISHES
SEA AND SEASHORE
GEOLOGY
ASTRONOMY
WEATHER
CATS
DOGS
HORSES AND PONIES

*Transport*
AIRCRAFT
AUTOMOBILES
COMMERCIAL VEHICLES
SHIPS
MANNED SPACEFLIGHT

*The Arts etc*
ARCHITECTURE
CATHEDRALS
CHURCHES
HERALDRY
FLAGS
PAINTING
MODERN ART
SCULPTURE
FURNITURE
MUSIC
POSTAGE STAMPS

*Sport*
ASSOCIATION FOOTBALL
CRICKET

*Cities*
LONDON

# CONTENTS

List of Colour Plates                        5

How to Use This Book                         7

Key Points                                   9

General Information                          13

Introduction                                15

Yesterday in Today's London                 21

Gazetteer                                   39

Index                                      185

# LIST OF COLOUR PLATES

*Plate 1*    View down the River Thames from County Hall

             Centre Point, a modern office block, and St Giles-in-the-Fields

*Plate 2*    Roof of Henry VII's Chapel, Westminster Abbey, showing fan vaulting

             The White Tower, the Norman keep of the Tower of London

*Plate 3*    The South Front of Hampton Court Palace, designed by Sir Christopher Wren

             Queen Charlotte's State Bedroom, Hampton Court Palace

*Plate 4*  The statue of Physical Energy, by G. F. Watts, Kensington Gardens

The Albert Memorial, Kensington Gardens

*Plate 5*  Parliament Square, with the Houses of Parliament and St Margaret, Westminster

The Commonwealth Institute

*Plate 6*  Petticoat Lane Market, Middlesex Street

Portobello Road Market

*Plate 7*  Canonbury Tower and Canonbury House, Islington

Shepherd Market, an attractive 'village' quarter off Piccadilly

*Plate 8*  Interior of St Stephen Walbrook, designed by Sir Christopher Wren

6

# HOW TO USE THIS BOOK

*The Observer's Book of London* is divided into two main parts:

YESTERDAY IN TODAY'S LONDON

GAZETTEER

**Yesterday in Today's London** describes what can still be seen of the London of the past, from Roman times up to the present century, and will be of value to those whose interests lie in a particular period of history.

**The Gazetteer**, which forms the greater part of the book, has entries for all the most important places of interest in London, including many less well-known sights which are as fascinating and worth visiting as some of the more famous ones.

In addition to the normal alphabetical entries, the gazetteer contains the following **group entries**: Architects; Bridges; City Churches; Commemorative Plaques; Inns of Court; Markets; Museums, Art Galleries and Collections; Railway Stations; Royal Parks; Statues. Any particular item in a group can be found by reference to the index. All entries are cross-referenced where necessary.

*The Gazetteer* does not claim to be fully comprehensive. For a book of this nature selection must be subjective, and compression and omissions are inevitable. The face of London is changing almost daily as new buildings, both public and private, go up and others come down, and it is impossible to guarantee that the text, though up to date at the time of publication, will not suffer from the rapidity of the changes. What it is hoped to provide is a stepping-stone to a view of London over the centuries, so that both the native and the visitor will be stimulated to delve deeper into London's history and to investigate in greater detail the many fascinating aspects of this extraordinary and romantic city.

Haymarket
Theatre

# KEY POINTS

The maps on the endpapers provide a number of **Key Points**, which are an important feature of the book. These **Key Points** have been placed at convenient intervals to make it possible for the visitor to use each one as the starting-point for a centre of interest, so that a particular area can be explored in such a way that both time and energy may be saved, and unnecessary journeys avoided. Of course, London cannot be fully explored in a day, a week, or a year. Lifelong devotees of the city are continually discovering some hitherto unknown spot or a new facet of London's history, and this is part of its charm. But for the visitor from the country or abroad, this suggested plan of choosing a **Key Point** and working outwards from it should provide a reasonably comprehensive coverage for those who want to see as much as possible in as short a time as possible.

Each **Key Point** is at or near an easily accessible traffic centre, and the journey from it may be taken on foot or by using the minimum of public transport. Those routes which are outside central London (and some of the **Key Points** are, for reasons of space, 'off the map') will need more time and planning. For instance, a trip to Hampstead or Greenwich should be undertaken on its own, and the few out of London places such as Hampton Court Palace, Ham House and Kew Gardens merit similar treatment. Many interesting places on the Thames can be seen on a trip by motor-launch: from Westminster Pier to the Tower of London; or to Greenwich, Putney, Kew, Richmond and Hampton Court.

*See overleaf.*

9

## ★ THE ANGEL, ISLINGTON
Camden Passage, Canonbury Tower, Sadler's Wells Theatre

## ★ BAKER STREET STATION
Madame Tussaud's, Planetarium, Regent's Park, Zoological Gardens

## ★ BANK STATION
Bank of England, Change Alley, Cheapside, College of Arms, Corn Exchange, Cornhill, Guildhall, Guildhall Museum, Leadenhall Market, Lloyd's, London Stone, Mansion House, Royal Exchange, St Andrew Undershaft, St Katherine Creechurch, St Lawrence Jewry, St Margaret Lothbury, St Mary Aldermary, St Mary Woolnoth, St Peter Cornhill, St Stephen Walbrook, Stock Exchange, Temple of Mithras

## ★ BARBICAN STATION
The Barbican, Charterhouse, Clerks' Well, Cock Lane, Ely Place, St Bartholomew-the-Great, St Botolph Aldersgate, St Giles Cripplegate, St John's Gate, Smithfield

## ★ BRITISH MUSEUM (Tottenham Court Road Station)
Bloomsbury, Congress House, Coram's Fields, Courtauld Institute Galleries, Dickens House, Jewish Museum, Percival David Foundation of Chinese Art, Pollock's Toy Museum, Post Office Tower, Wellcome Institute, University of London

## ★ COVENT GARDEN STATION
Covent Garden Theatre, Drury Lane Theatre, Roman Bath, St Paul's Covent Garden, Somerset House

## ★ FLEET STREET (Temple or St Paul's Station)
Cheshire Cheese, Dr Johnson's House, Gray's Inn, Inner Temple, Lincoln's Inn, Lincoln's Inn Fields, London Silver Vaults, Middle Temple, Old Curiosity Shop, Prince Henry's Room, Public Records Office, Royal Courts of Justice, St Andrew Holborn, St Bride Fleet Street, St Clement Danes, St Dunstan-in-the-West, Sir John Soane's Museum, Staple Inn, Temple Bar

**★ GREENWICH** (Greenwich or Maze Hill, British Rail)
*Cutty Sark, Gipsy Moth IV*, Greenwich Park, National Maritime Museum, Old Royal Observatory, Queen's House, Royal Naval College

**★ HAMPSTEAD STATION**
Fenton House (Benton-Fletcher Collection and Binning Collection), Hampstead Heath, Keats House, Kenwood House

**★ HYDE PARK CORNER**
Apsley House, Buckingham Palace, Green Park, Queen's Gallery, Royal Mews

**★ LIVERPOOL STREET STATION**
All Hallows, London Wall, Bunhill Fields, Club Row, Geffrye Museum, Petticoat Lane, St Ethelburga Bishopsgate, St Helen Bishopsgate, Spanish and Portuguese Synagogue, Wesley's House

**★ LONDON BRIDGE STATION**
Bankside, Bear Gardens Museum, Cuming Museum, George Inn, Southwark Cathedral

**★ MARBLE ARCH**
Courtauld Institute of Art, Grosvenor Square, Speakers' Corner, Tyburn Tree, Wallace Collection

**★ MONUMENT**
Custom House, Billingsgate, London Bridge, St James Garlickhythe, St Magnus the Martyr, St Margaret Pattens, St Mary Abchurch, St Mary-at-Hill, St Michael Paternoster Royal

**★ PARLIAMENT SQUARE** (Westminster Station)
Big Ben, Birdcage Walk, Cenotaph, Downing Street, Houses of Parliament, Jewel Tower, New Scotland Yard, St Margaret Westminster, Westminster Abbey, Westminster Bridge, Westminster Cathedral

11

### ★ PICCADILLY CIRCUS
Berwick Market, Bond Street, Broadcasting House, Burlington Arcade, Burlington House, Carnaby Street, Eros, Haymarket Theatre, House of St Barnabas, Lancaster House, Leicester Square, Regent Street, St James Piccadilly, Soho

### ★ QUEENSWAY STATION
Elfin Oak, Kensington Gardens, Kensington Palace, London Museum, Portobello Road

### ★ ST PAUL'S STATION
Blackfriars Bridge, Central Criminal Court, National Postal Museum, St Andrew-by-the-Wardrobe, St Benet Paul's Wharf, St Martin Ludgate, St Mary-le-Bow, St Paul's Cathedral, St Sepulchre-without-Newgate, St Vedas Foster Lane

### ★ SLOANE SQUARE STATION
Carlyle's House, Chelsea Old Church, Chelsea Royal Hospital, Crosby Hall, National Army Museum

### ★ SOUTH KENSINGTON STATION
Albert Hall, Albert Memorial, Brompton Oratory, Donaldson Collection (Royal College of Music), Geological Museum, Natural History Museum, Science Museum, Victoria and Albert Museum

### ★ TOWER HILL STATION
All Hallows Barking-by-the-Tower, HMS *Belfast*, St Olave Hart Street, Tower Bridge, Tower of London

### ★ TRAFALGAR SQUARE
Adelphi, Admiralty, Admiralty Arch, Banqueting House, Carlton House Terrace, Charing Cross, Cleopatra's Needle, HMS *Discovery*, Duke of York's Column, Guards Crimea Memorial, Henry VIII's Wine Cellar, Horse Guards, The Mall, Marlborough House, National Gallery, National Portrait Gallery, Nelson's Column, Pall Mall, Royal Opera Arcade, Royal Society of Arts, St James's Palace, St James's Park, St Martin-in-the-Fields, Savoy Chapel, Strand

★ **WATERLOO STATION**

County Hall, Hayward Gallery, Imperial War Museum, Lambeth Palace, Old Vic Theatre, Royal Festival Hall, South Bank, South Bank Lion, Waterloo Bridge

One of Landseer's lions.
Trafalgar Square

# GENERAL INFORMATION

The following points should be taken into consideration when planning visits:

Museums, Galleries and Collections usually close on Sunday mornings. The Central Criminal Court, County Hall and the Houses of Parliament are normally open on Saturdays only. The Royal Mews is open on Wednesdays and Thursdays; Lancaster House on Saturdays and Sundays. The Jewish Museum closes on Saturdays. Dickens House, Dr Johnson's House, the Guildhall Museum, Keats House and Leighton House close on Sundays. The National Postal Museum and the Public Record Office are closed on Saturdays and Sundays. Sir John Soane's Museum is closed on Sundays and Mondays. The Geffrye Museum and the Queen's Gallery close on Mondays;

Carlyle's House and Fenton House on Tuesdays; the Jewel Tower on Wednesdays and the Royal Naval College on Thursdays. The Tower of London is closed on Sundays in winter. The Roman Bath is open on weekdays, mornings only.

The Mansion House and Henry VIII's Wine Cellar are open on Saturday afternoons, and permits are necessary; this applies also to Charterhouse. Advance permission is needed for entrance to the Royal College of Music and St John's Gate.

The City Churches are normally open from Monday to Friday, though some can be visited only during the middle of the day. Many are closed on Sundays.

The City Information Centre in St Paul's Churchyard (01–606 3030) is an invaluable source for more detailed information about City matters. The National Book League, 7 Albemarle Street, W1 (01–493 9001) publishes a booklet which contains a very comprehensive list of books about London, its history, architecture, pageantry, pastimes and arts, as well as guides and maps. From the Greater London Council Bookshop at County Hall (01–633 8849) a number of interesting publications, maps and prints are available.

Free maps of the Underground and bus services can be obtained from any London Transport ticket office or Enquiry office.

# INTRODUCTION

The history of London, from bridge-point to the metropolis of today, spans more than nineteen centuries, but by the standards of some Mediterranean towns London is relatively young. There were settlements of Iron Age people along the banks of the Thames before the Romans arrived, but these had not been concentrated. The Romans were quick to see the natural advantages the site had to offer, as this was the first point at which the Thames was fordable. The river served as a frontier and a highway, and London became a well-sited port facing the Continent, a centre for the waterborne trade of the Thames and Lea valleys, and the hub of a road system that embraced the whole of England. The town was not only the junction of a series of main roads, but afforded protection to those who crossed the broad river.

At first the Romans did not make the walled city their seat of government, even though it was the largest city in Britain and the fifth largest in Europe. They used it as a major port, and Tacitus noted that it was 'packed with traders'. Life in Roman London was rich and sophisticated, and the buildings were large and splendid. Before the end of the 1st century it became the capital.

When the Romans left the country in the 5th century AD, the Saxon invaders overran London and destroyed almost every trace of Roman civilization. However, London appears never to have been completely abandoned. It survived the Anglo-Saxons, and eventually a new city arose.

In the time of Alfred the Great, London was a strongly fortified town, though it was not the seat of government. It was after the Norman Conquest that London became the centre of royal administration, with the Royal Treasury, the Supreme Court and Parliament all sited at Westminster.

The Tower, built by William the Conqueror to show his supreme power, was fortress, prison and mint. A new stone London Bridge was the connection with Southwark, an area which expanded on the other side of the Thames. During the next 400 years merchants grew rich in cloth, tin, wine, leather and metals. St Paul's Cathedral and the many churches and fraternities, both inside and outside the City walls, catered for all religious needs. At this time learning flourished, and Chaucer wrote *The Canterbury Tales*. Further impetus was given by the invention of the printing press and London soon established a near monopoly of printing.

When the Tudor monarchs reigned, between 1485 and 1603, great changes took place. A strong central government kept the country at peace for most of the time, and the discovery of America, and the sea route to India and China meant that England became well placed for the new overseas trade routes. Whereas England had been on the edge of world events, it was now at the centre. The weakening of the Italian city-states, under attack from France and Spain, brought trade to a more stable city. When the monasteries were dissolved large areas of land were available for agriculture and building. A number of royal palaces were erected along the Thames: Greenwich, Westminster, Whitehall, St James's, Hampton Court, Richmond and Windsor, and the grounds of some of them have subsequently become the parks that are so numerous in and around London today. The expansion of trade was given another fillip by the influx of protestant Flemings and Frenchmen, whose money and skills were eagerly sought, even though the refugees themselves were unpopular. Craft guilds increased in power and wealth. In spite of plagues and diseases the population rose rapidly.

By now London was prosperous, and material prosperity went hand in hand with enthusiasm for learning. With the opening of schools and the opportunities given by wealthy patrons, social and cultural standards were higher than they had ever been since Roman times.

Stuart London continued the Tudor trend, in spite of the Civil War and the break in monarchical government, but there were developments on different lines. The first planned developments of whole areas were started, beginning with Covent Garden, and the fashion for squares lasted for the next 200 years. Between the City and Westminster, nobles and courtiers had large estates on which they built sumptuous mansions; in fact, grand town houses were everywhere. The Port of London increased its activities and operated further and further along both sides of the river.

But London was not a healthy place to live in, and disease reached a peak in 1665 when perhaps 100,000 Londoners died of bubonic plague. In 1666 four-fifths of the City was destroyed by fire, including most of the medieval churches. Yet in five years, such was the attraction of the capital, the importance of the port and the value of the accumulated wealth of the City merchants that the City was full of people again, broader streets and brick buildings had been built, and improvements made in the layout of large areas. Church building followed. St Paul's Cathedral and many of the City churches were designed by Christopher Wren, though his plan for the development of a new London came to nothing; opposition from property owners was too strong.

At this time the first London newspapers appeared and were struggling for freedom of expression, and men everywhere were beginning to resent authority. There was much tension between the City and the Crown. It was the power of the City that opposed Charles I, supplied men and money in the fight against the king's autocracy, kept Cromwell in power, made Charles II king, and helped William of Orange to come to the throne.

During the next hundred years London continued to grow, and many new houses, roads and bridges were built. Business matters and current affairs were discussed in the coffee houses; pamphleteers and newspapers disseminated news and influenced public opinion. London was now a world capital, drawing wealth from trade all round the globe.

In the 19th century London outgrew itself. The population increased alarmingly, and the public services, such as they were, became totally inadequate. The housing problem was acute. New docks and bridges were needed; water supplies and sewers had to be provided. There was a major innovation in transport: canals, railways, and later buses, tramways and underground railways eased congestion for a time. Because of overcrowding and the appalling poverty of the underprivileged there was a great strain on law and order, and this led to the formation of the Metropolitan Police Force. Philanthropists took up the cudgels for the poor and needy; stringent building regulations came into force and housing schemes for the poor were introduced. Craftsmanship, which had been a feature of English life for centuries, was supplemented and eventually superseded by mass production. The Industrial Revolution transformed England from an agricultural country into an industrial and urban one, and London found itself caught up in the great upheaval.

But as the century wore on London managed to adapt itself to some of the problems that its size and population had caused. Local government was reorganized; organized labour slowly emerged in struggles against the indifference and greed of capitalism, and some of the worst aspects of the general poverty were alleviated by the stirrings of the Victorian conscience, voiced among others by Dickens, Ruskin and Morris.

The present century relieved some of the problems and provided new ones. It saw the development of the suburbs and the beginnings of the urban sprawl, and the upsurge of property developers and speculative builders who are becoming more powerful and causing more concern every year. The First World War halted London's expansion temporarily; casualties then were human beings rather than bricks and stone. Ribbon development and 'by-pass Tudor' houses were unattractive features of building between the wars, but the establishment of the Green Belt did something to halt this expansion. The Second World War caused a real setback in London's progress. Much of the City was devastated. Churches, shops, offices and streets of houses disappeared overnight. After the war rebuilding was slow, owing to economic difficulties, and is still unfinished.

After the grey austerity of the post-war years, London's vitality and irrepressible optimism are reasserting themselves. London still remains the main target for the business world even though firms are being encouraged to move out to the new towns. It is still the commercial and banking metropolis of the

Commonwealth, even if it is no longer the hub of an empire, and it is one of the chief centres of population and prosperity in the world. It still remains a great port, a social centre and administrative capital. Music, art and literature flourish in London as they do in no other place. Though strangled by cars and disrupted by trunk roads, London is still one of the world's most interesting cities. It is a storehouse of fine architecture, and retains many fascinating links with all that has gone to make up its long history.

Everywhere, and often in the most unexpected places, there is evidence of the artistry and skill of designers and craftsmen of bygone ages, and of the way in which people of both high and low degree lived. It is still easy, when wandering about London's streets, squares, alleys and courts, to be temporarily transported into a slower, more elegant, less harassing age. It is dangerous, not to say impossible, to live in the past, but the past can often be a useful corrective to the present; and London provides that corrective in abundance.

Arms of the City of London

Mithras slaying the bull, London Museum

# YESTERDAY IN TODAY'S LONDON

## Roman London

London started to develop when the Romans laid out their military roads in south-east Britain soon after their invasion of AD 43. Originally it was little more than a settlement of merchants and officials situated to the east of a small tributary of the Thames called the Walbrook. Soon it spread to the western side of the stream, and eventually became the largest city in Roman Britain—the centre of financial administration and the capital.

The construction of a large fort to the north-west of the city in the middle of the 2nd century emphasizes its importance, though the fort was designed probably for the local enforcement of law and to house ceremonial troops, and was not built for any strategic purpose. About AD 200 the city was enclosed by a defensive wall, covering an area of about 330 acres, to which bastions were later added. The line of the wall from the Tower of London to Ludgate runs north-ward from the Wardrobe Tower region of the Tower of London to the line of Jewry Street and then to Aldgate. From there it passes under the line of Duke's Place to Bishopsgate, continuing in a westerly direction parallel to Wormwood Street, underneath the line of the modern London Wall to a point just past Moorgate. It then continues westward past Wood Street, where it becomes part of the Cripplegate Fort area.

The wall then swings south-south-west, runs parallel to Noble Street to the corner of Oat Lane and turns west across Aldersgate Street to the most westerly bastion below the Post Office yard. Here it veers south past Newgate Street and the west end of Amen Court, to finish in the neighbourhood of Queen Victoria Street, where it originally reached the Thames.

Much of the wall that remained was swept away by the Commissioner of Sewers in 1766, and the parts now easily accessible are few but interesting. The remains of the medieval Wardrobe Tower incorporate the base of a Roman tower apparently hollow, of U-shaped plan. This base of rubble masonry with a double bonding course of tiles set in pink mortar is five feet high. There is also a ten-feet length of wall nearly five feet high at the back of the Wardrobe Tower. In the Wakefield Gardens almost the whole of the wall above ground is medieval, but the lower courses are Roman. Here again the layers of red bonding bricks can be seen.

In the basement of the Toc H Club in Trinity Square a stretch of the external face of the wall extends the full length of the room. Behind Midland House in Cooper's Row the wall is 35 feet high. The upper part is medieval, but the base is Roman and shows the usual squared ragstone separated by courses of red bonding tiles. In the underground car park under the western part of London Wall is a fine stretch of the

(*above*) Bastion of medieval wall, Barbican
(*below*) Temple of Mithras

23

wall, with sandstone plinth and levelling brick courses; in one place it is six feet high.

The north carriageway of the west gate of the Roman Cripplegate Fort, and its adjoining guard chamber, together with a short stretch of fort wall, is preserved in an underground room at the west end of London Wall. Remains of the reinforcing masonry, added inside the fort wall when it was incorporated into the defensive wall, may also be seen. Other stretches of the fort and city wall are visible from street level in Noble Street, where there are remains of a rectangular turret at the south-west corner of the fort, at St Giles, Cripplegate, where the medieval wall and bastion survive to a height of about 20 feet and are built on Roman foundations, and in St Alphage's Churchyard, where again the bottom of this stretch is Roman.

In a court on the east side of the Old Bailey a fragment of the lower part of the wall, chiefly medieval, is preserved, and a long stretch with a hollow angle-bastion survives in the basement of the Post Office buildings in King Edward Street. Another fragment is preserved in Warwick Square, off Warwick Lane, between Newgate Street and Ludgate Hill; this was exposed during work on the former premises of the Oxford University Press.

Turning to other Roman remains—in the crypt of All Hallows Barking by-the-Tower is a red tessellated pavement, and a display of Roman pottery and other finds. At the bottom of the staircase near the Threadneedle Street entrance to the Bank of England is a mosaic pavement of the late 2nd or early 3rd century. It has been greatly restored and relaid, though not on its original site. Another patterned mosaic pavement, probably belonging to the late 3rd century, can be seen in the basement of the offices at 11 Ironmonger Lane. In the crypt of St Bride's, off Fleet Street, a plain red tessellated pavement can be seen reflected in a mirror. This was part of the only building definitely established as Roman that has been found between the City and Westminster.

The remains of the Temple of Mithras, which stood beside the River Walbrook, were unearthed in 1954. They were transferred from their original site and can now be seen on the Queen Victoria Street frontage of Temple Court.

No study of Roman London would be complete without visits to the Guildhall, London and British Museums. The Guildhall Museum shows the development of the 'square mile' from the earliest times. Exhibits are arranged in three separate rooms, two of them being concerned with Roman London. The first contains antiquities illustrating Roman religion, and particularly important are the finds from the Temple of Mithras. The second room traces the origins of the city and its life under Roman rule. Among the many items connected with trade is a horse-powered grain mill. Household equipment is illustrated by a range of articles from ordinary cooking pots to imported glass vessels. There is a wooden ladder, some leather 'bikini' pants found in a well in Queen Street, craftsmen's tools, cutlery, coins and articles of adornment.

The main items of Roman interest in the London Museum are writing and weighing implements, tools, surgical and toilet instruments, London-minted coins, pottery, lamps, statuettes and a flagon, ten inches high, inscribed *Londini ad fanum Isidis* (In London by the Temple of Isis): this is the earliest known example of an inscription in which the Roman name for London occurs. There is also part of a mosaic floor about three feet square which came from a building near the Walbrook, where the Mansion House now stands. The remains of a Roman boat, 38 feet long, now in the museum, were discovered when the site of County Hall was being excavated.

In the British Museum there is a tombstone of

Procurator Classicianus; a round mosaic of Bacchus on a tiger, from Leadenhall Street; a bronze head of Hadrian; a silver ingot from the Tower of London; bronze statuettes; an inscribed stone memorial; items of adornment; a model ship's prow; writing implements and a porphyry cinerary urn.

In the Chapter House of Westminster Abbey is a sarcophagus that was found on the north side of the green. The inscription tells us that it is in memory of Valerius Amandus, and was made by Valerius Superventor and Valerius Marcellus for their father. The cross it bears may have been added in Saxon times.

The Cuming Museum in Southwark has many interesting exhibits that have been found to the south of the Thames.

## Anglo-Saxon London

The withdrawal of the Romans from Britain, and the consequent collapse of both government and trade, meant that only a small population was able to subsist in the once flourishing city of London, protected by its walls. The first Saxon bishop of London was ordained in AD 604, and the city was by then probably largely independent, beginning to stir itself and regain its confidence. In the 7th century it was producing its own coins, and a hundred years later trade was flourishing and the Romans were forgotten.

London came under attack from the Vikings, and the fortifications were repaired by Alfred the Great, after which the city was able to offer strong resistance to the invaders. It grew in political importance as well as in military strength, and in 1016 Edmund was chosen by his peers and the citizens of London to be king. An honourable peace was made with the Danes, who had won nearly the whole of the rest of the country, and London was by then so prosperous that it was able to give to the Danes an eighth part of the total levy which they demanded from the whole nation.

Few objects survive from Saxon London, but in the third room of the Guildhall Museum is a fine relief depicting a lion, with a runic inscription, from St Paul's Churchyard, probably carved in the 10th century. There are also some amber beads, a chatelaine for carrying housekeeping keys, a range of spearheads, a hoard of jewellery found in Cheapside, a cooking pot, a bone comb, some loom weights and parts of drinking horns.

In the London Museum are Anglo-Saxon and Danish swords, Viking horse equipment, a large bell, bone chessmen and counters, combs, spoons, and a hoard from a Viking ship which was involved in a battle near London Bridge. This consists of battle-axes, spearheads, a grappling-iron, smith's tongs, axes, knives and pots.

The Manuscript Room of the British Museum displays illuminated manuscripts of the period, including Bede's *Ecclesiastical History of the English Nation*, the Bosworth Psalter, written in 10th-century Latin, with Anglo-Saxon between the lines in small print, and the *Anglo-Saxon Chronicle* of the 11th century.

Though not of London origin, the magnificent assembly of grave goods of a 7th-century Saxon king, dug up near Ipswich in 1939 and called the Sutton Hoo Treasure, is of outstanding importance—the richest treasure ever to be found in Britain.

The apse of a Saxon church can be seen in the crypt of St Bride's, off Fleet Street, and another in the crypt of All Hallows Barking by-the-Tower, where parts of a Saxon cross have also been found.

The Cuming Museum has a grappling-iron found near London Bridge.

## Norman and Medieval London

After the Norman Conquest the life style of London was little disturbed. The city gained in both power and ambition; its corporate unity grew with its wealth, so that gradually it secured autonomous rule and had the responsibility of supervising almost every aspect of local government. Commerce depended on the Thames, and the river front was the most crowded part of the city.

Most of the citizens were engaged in handicrafts and retail trades, though others were concerned with overseas trade and many became rich. By the 14th century wealthy merchants were able to build large mansions, copying those of the nobility. They also added to the architectural splendour of the Tower of London, London Bridge, St Paul's Cathedral, the 100 parish churches and the 23 monastic establishments. In the late 12th century the Palace of Westminster became the centre of a complex of government departments, courts and colleges of law, and by the end of the 14th century the centre of the country's literary and social scene was in London.

Of Norman London there are, in many categories, few remains. There is virtually no Norman armour anywhere in the country, but there are swords of the period in the Tower of London, and suits of mail which are similar to those worn by the Normans.

The Domesday Book, in two volumes, which contains the results of the detailed survey on England, commissioned by William the Conqueror for the purpose of tax assessment, is kept in the Public Record Office in Chancery Lane.

Norman buildings in London include St Bartholomew-the-Great, West Smithfield, the oldest surviving church in the City. It is a fine example of Norman architecture with its massive columns and rounded arches. St Mary-le-Bow in Cheapside stands above an early Norman crypt, all that is left of the original church, and the stone arches, or bows, have given the church its name; in medieval times it was called St Maria-de-Arcubus. Another Norman crypt is that

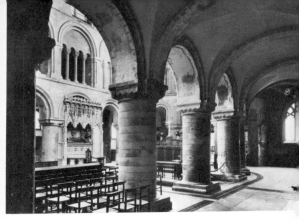

St Bartholomew the Great: interior showing Norman work

of St John's Priory, Clerkenwell, founded by the Knights Hospitallers of St John of Jerusalem about 1100, again all that is left of the original building.

Within the Temple (comprised of two Inns of Court) is the Temple Church, consecrated in 1185, and an excellent example of Norman Transitional style, the round nave being pure Norman and the chancel Early English. On the floor are 12th- and 13th-century effigies of Knights of the Order of Knights Templars, and on the capitals of the columns around the wall a Norman stonemason carved many grotesque faces.

The White Tower, the oldest part of the Tower of London, is the stone keep. It was begun in about 1078 and replaced the old wooden motte-and-bailey. The Chapel of St John, on the second floor, is its most interesting feature; it is the oldest example of Norman religious architecture. The arches and pillars of the nave are characteristic Norman work, so are the simple barrel vault over the clerestory and the five stilted arches connecting the apse to an ambulatory.

Southwark Cathedral still retains a few traces of the great Norman church that was destroyed by fire in 1206. There are remains of an arch through the door to the vestry, the north transept is Norman and so are the arches to the Harvard Chapel; there is a wooden effigy of a Crusader in the north choir aisle.

In Westminster Abbey the only surviving Norman parts are the Chamber of the Pyx, first a sacristy and later the royal treasury, and the Undercroft, which now houses the Abbey Museum.

Westminster Hall, the Great Hall of the Palace of Westminster, was originally built by William Rufus, son of William the Conqueror, about 1090, but was altered considerably by Richard II 300 years later.

In the Victoria and Albert Museum are several fine examples of 11th- and 12th-century craftsmanship: carvings in bone and whalebone, the Gloucester Candlestick, the Narwhal Horn, and a leaf from a Psalter from between 1130 and 1150. In the London Museum there are knives and keys of the period, a decorated bowl of the 12th century, a decorated leather sheaf, and a cresset lamp made from a 12th-century

Effigies of Crusader Knights, Temple Church

capital. The Guildhall Museum has bone chessmen of the 12th and 13th centuries, arrow-heads and a cooking pot. In the King Edward VII Gallery of the British Museum the Norman remains include ivory chessmen, a portable altar, a bronze bowl and some pottery.

Most of the fabric of medieval London was destroyed in the Great Fire of 1666, but about 20 buildings, mainly ecclesiastical, survive, and they form an important and varied body of medieval architecture.

The Jewel Tower, across the road from the Victoria Tower of the Houses of Parliament, was built in 1365–6, and was used as a treasury for the Crown Jewels, later becoming the repository for Parliament's official archives. Together with Westminster Hall it survived the fire which destroyed the rest of the palace.

Eltham Palace, of which only the hall still stands, has a fine medieval hammer-beam roof. It was built by Edward IV, succeeding one erected by Henry VI.

London churches which contain work of the Early English Period (1150–1300), the Decorated Period (1270–1400) and the Perpendicular Period (1350–1550) include: the Lady Chapel at the east end of St Bartholomew-the-Great, though restored in 1330; St Etheldreda's Church in Ely Place, Holborn; the Undercroft of St Stephen's Chapel in the Houses of Parliament; the chancel of the Temple Church with its lancet-shaped windows and linear thinness of form; the choir of Southwark Cathedral, which is partly the remains and partly a copy of the priory church of St Mary Overy; part of St Helen's, Bishopsgate, which has two naves separated by an arcade; the Henry VII Chapel in Westminster Abbey, and the austere octagonal shell of the Chapter House with its original floor tiles; and St Margaret, Westminster, in Late Perpendicular style, though restored in the 18th century.

In Guildhall most of the interior of the porch is

medieval, as is the stone shell of the hall; a window in the south wall survives from the 15th century, with some panes of horn instead of glass. The magnificently vaulted crypt is an example of domestic Perpendicular architecture. Archbishop Morton's gatehouse at Lambeth Palace belongs to the same period. In the Gresham Street and Wood Street area around Guildhall are some metal plaques, relics of medieval times, that carry the coats of arms of the Goldsmiths' and Haberdashers' Livery Companies which own property in the district.

## Tudor London

In the early 16th century London was still a walled city. There were 23 wards within the gates and two wards without, to which part of Southwark was later added. The city was governed by the Lord Mayor and his aldermen, though economic activities were controlled by the Livery Companies. The City of Westminster, comprising the Abbey precinct and the palaces of Westminster, St James and Whitehall, was separated from the City by the fields of Holborn and Charing Cross. Westminster had become the seat of the Court, Parliament and the Courts of Justice. West of the Temple were the great Tudor mansions. By about 1600 the population of London was over 200,000, though the numbers of those actually living within the walls had decreased. New buildings took over much of the open space within and without the city and spread into the country—to Shoreditch, Whitechapel, Wapping, and south of the river along Bankside. Neither proclamation, statute, nor disease could check the growth of London.

The Thames was still the principal thoroughfare, and only London Bridge spanned it. The Pool of London became the greatest port in the country, and London merchants promoted enterprises in which seamen sailed over every sea to almost every country.

What London looked like in Tudor times can best
be seen from the drawings, maps and plans in the
British Museum, the Guildhall Library, the London
Museum and the Public Record Office. The earliest
printed plan of London (or fragments of a plan), drawn
between 1553 and 1559, is in the London Museum.
The two extant copperplates show an area from the
river north to Finsbury Fields and from Bow Church
to Houndsditch. They are rich in pictorial illustra-
tions of buildings and show scenes of social life drawn
in perspective, revealing the distribution of buildings and open spaces.

In the British Museum, John Norden's plans of
London and Westminster (1593) are the first to illus-
trate the rapid growth of the city in the reign of
Elizabeth I, and show the ribbon development along
the highways into the countryside beyond the gates.
There is also a pen-and-ink and watercolour picture

by R. Treswell in 1585 of West Cheap, the greatest market in Tudor London; a plan by William Hayward and John Gascoyne of the Tower of London in 1597; and a view of the Pool of London about 1600.

The Guildhall Library contains the first edition of John Stow's *Survey of London* (1598), which is a vital document for information about the topography and antiquities of the Elizabethan city. Also in Guildhall is the earliest surviving bill of mortality for London, for the year 1582. The practice of recording weekly and monthly burials in London parishes began in the 16th century, apparently in time of plague. There is also a manuscript chronicle of the City of London from 1189 to 1512, the main portion of which was written towards the end of the 15th century and completed in 1512, probably by Robert Fabyan, draper and alderman. It contains corrections and additions by John Stow. A proclamation by Elizabeth I, dated 1580, to prohibit building in the City and its immediate vicinity shows how the growth of London's population had outstripped accommodation, and how outbreaks of plague could spread rapidly in the crowded conditions prevailing at the time.

The Public Record Office has a 1542 manuscript plan of Borough High Street in Southwark. Some of the many inns in the street, one of the oldest in the London area, appear in the plan, and a pillory is also shown.

Among the Tudor buildings, or parts of them (many are much restored), that still survive are: Barnard's Inn, Holborn; the Canonbury Tower in Islington; Charterhouse; the More Chapel and two capitals in Chelsea Old Church; Crosby Hall; the gateway and quadrangle of Fulham Palace; the older parts of Hampton Court Palace; Henry VIII's Wine Cellar under the head office of the Ministry of Defence in Whitehall; Middle Temple Hall; the Great Hall of Gray's Inn; the Old Curiosity Shop in Portsmouth

Street; parts of St James's Palace; St John's Gate in Clerkenwell; the Savoy Chapel; Staple Inn, Holborn. There is Tudor work in the church of St Andrew Undershaft in Leadenhall Street; St Dunstan in-the-West, where there is a contemporary statue of Elizabeth I over the vestry door; the tower of St Katherine Creechurch; St Margaret, Westminster; the altar screen of Southwark Cathedral; the Henry VII Chapel in Westminster Abbey; the Queen's House in the Tower of London—the residence of the Governor.

## From 17th-century to 20th-century London

In spite of the devastation caused by the Great Fire of 1666, 17th-century monuments of all kinds abound. Starting with Inigo Jones's contributions to London's architecture—the Queen's House at Greenwich, the Banqueting House of Whitehall Palace, and the Queen's Chapel facing St James's Palace—the century, with the exception of the Commonwealth period, was a time of great magnificence. It culminated in the new city for which Sir Christopher Wren was chiefly responsible, with St Paul's Cathedral at the centre, rising like a giant star amid a host of lesser but equally beautiful ones. At the same time, the reconstruction of the major institutional and secular buildings was also undertaken: Chelsea Hospital, houses in King's Bench Walk, the Temple, Kensington Palace and Hampton Court, the Royal Naval College and Royal Observatory at Greenwich, Temple Bar and Marlborough House.

By 1700 London was fairly densely built up along the north bank of the Thames and still dependent on the river for its prosperity, though wheelborne traffic was increasing and social life was moving westwards. At this time James Gibbs and Nicholas Hawksmoor contributed their own versions of Baroque architecture to the growing elegance of the city with such churches as St Martin-in-the-Fields and St Mary Woolnoth, and with the addition of towers to Westminster Abbey. William Kent's decorations added lustre to many great houses—Kensington Palace and Hampton Court—to the Horse Guards, the Treasury buildings, and the gardens of Chiswick House. George Dance and his son supervised building activities in the City, principally the Mansion House, the façade of Guildhall, and Newgate Prison.

Later in the 18th century Sir William Chambers and the Adam brothers added to the London scene with Somerset House, Kew Gardens, the Adelphi, Apsley House, Kenwood House and Syon House. John Nash's lovely curves swept across London from Regent's Park to Carlton House Terrace.

But the rural atmosphere of London became threatened by the expansion of urban development in the 19th century. The City and Westminster were linked with former villages such as Chelsea, Kensington and Islington. Commerce spread down the river following the line of the docks, and the East End, once a fashionable adjunct of the City, was given over to streets of terraced working-class houses which later degenerated into slums. There was an increasing standardization of houses everywhere; the face of London lost some of its elegance and tended to become plain and uninspiring.

The Victorians also built solidly, in a wide variety of over-ornate styles: Classical, Renaissance and Gothic. In the first part of the 19th century areas such as Belgravia, west of Buckingham Palace, and St John's Wood were developed. Later came the Albert Hall, the Albert Memorial, the new Houses of Parliament (rebuilt after a fire), the British Museum, St Pancras Station Hotel, the Commonwealth Office, Foreign Office and Home Office, and in late Victorian times the New Admiralty, Brompton Oratory, the new wings of Burlington House and Westminster Cathedral.

The end of the 19th century and the beginning of the 20th was the age of the great hotels, of the Oxford Street stores, of banks and theatres—all part of the expression of London's wealth. After the First World War architecture remained essentially Edwardian. The City became more and more depopulated, owing to the rise of prices and rents, and people went to live in the outlying suburbs. Few of the 'modern' buildings of the 1920s and 1930s are of great interest. The Senate House of the University of London was built at this time, and examples of good commercial building are the Peter Jones department store in Sloane Square and Simpson's shop in Piccadilly.

In 1945 the opportunity for rebuilding London was greater than after the Great Fire of 1666 but, as then, lack of money and bureaucratic restrictions have prevented some of the developments from being carried out. Even so, in the last 25 years London has changed more rapidly than ever before in its history. Skyscraper blocks such as Centre Point, the Barbican, Vickers Building and many others have turned the city into a vertical rather than a horizontal one. Some of this modern architecture is beautiful as well as functional; much is unattractive, but it all reflects the state of transition that London is in.

Old
Temple
Bar

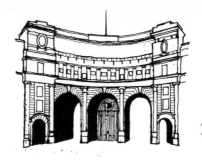

# GAZETTEER

The **Adelphi**, south of the Strand, was a speculative
building programme planned by three of the four
Adam brothers between 1768 and 1791. Land had
to be reclaimed from the Thames, and great arched
vaults served as foundations for the houses nearer the
river. One of these vaults can still be seen, for Robert
Street runs down to the Embankment from a cul-de-
sac called York Buildings, and is reached by an opening which leads into the cellars under the Adelphi.

Little of the original architecture remains, however,
as Adelphi Terrace was demolished in 1936 and replaced by a large block of office buildings. The former elegance of the district can be seen in the office of
the *Lancet* in Adam Street and the restored Royal
Society of Arts building in John Adam Street.

The **Admiralty** consists of two buildings. The
Old Admiralty, on the west side of Whitehall, SW1, was
designed by Thomas Ripley and erected in 1722-6.
A fine Robert Adam stone screen of 1761 masks a tall
classical portico in a small courtyard. The New
Admiralty, built in 1895 in the Italian Palladian style,

is in St James's Park, behind the old building, and is connected on the north side with the Admiralty Arch.

**Admiralty Arch**, sw1, at the Trafalgar Square end of the Mall, was built in 1910 as part of the national monument to Queen Victoria. Wrought-iron gates, designed by Sir Aston Webb, guard its triple arch, the centre one being opened only for Royal processions. Above the arch is part of the Admiralty's Library.

The **Albert Hall**, Kensington, sw7, capable of seating more than 8,000 people, is a huge oval amphitheatre with a glass dome, and it dominates Kensington Gore. It is used for concerts, meetings, displays and reunions, and for boxing and wrestling. The hall was built in 1867–71 on the site of Gore House, was designed by Captain Francis Fowke and cost £200,000. Queen Victoria opened it in 1871 and named it after her Consort. The terracotta frieze around it illustrates the triumphs of Art and Science, and bears witness to the Victorian regard for education and culture.

Inside there are three tiers of boxes (the initial cost was partly raised by the sale of boxes for £1,000 and £500 each), with a balcony and gallery above them. The organ has nearly 10,000 pipes.

The **Albert Memorial**, a Gothic extravaganza situated in Kensington Gardens, opposite the Albert Hall, was designed by Gilbert Scott, who was later knighted for his achievement. It was unveiled by Queen Victoria in 1876 as a memorial to her late husband. Scott based his design on the Eleanor crosses which marked the funeral route of Edward I's wife from Harby (Nottinghamshire) to London. In the tall spire there are statues representing such revered Victorian qualities as Faith, Hope, Charity, Chastity and Temperance, and beneath an ornate canopy in gilt and enamelled metal, a 15-foot tall Prince Albert sits, holding in one hand a catalogue of the Great Exhibition of 1851—his brain-child.

**Apsley House** (Wellington Museum), 149 Piccadilly, w1, on Hyde Park Corner, was known as 'Number One London' when town gave way to open country at that point. The house belonged to the Duke of Wellington from 1817 until his death in 1852. It was originally a red-brick Adam building, but the outside was refaced with Bath stone and the inside lushly redecorated by Benjamin Wyatt between 1828 and 1830. A Corinthian portico was added, and also the Waterloo Gallery. The house was acquired by the nation in 1947 and opened as the Wellington Museum in 1952. It is administered by the Victoria and Albert Museum.

Apsley House contains many of the Duke's personal relics, orders and decorations and rewards of victory. There is a 15-foot high figure of Napoleon carved by Canova, a portrait by Wilkie of George IV in a kilt, and a magnificent chandelier in the Waterloo Gallery. This gallery also contains the ornate Portuguese Service laid out on the original banqueting table. The Striped Drawing-room has fine portraits of some of Wellington's generals, and busts of the Younger Pitt and Spencer Perceval. There are paintings by Velasquez, Rubens, Murillo and Correggio, and Lawrence's portrait of the Duke.

## ARCHITECTS

**Adam, Robert** (1728–92) was born in Scotland and is the best known of four brothers who all became architects and designers. In 1762 he became architect to George III, but resigned in 1768 to enter Parliament. With two of his brothers he planned and built the Adelphi, off the Strand. Robert Adam was responsible for the interior decoration of the houses, and his influence generally was felt more in domestic design than in architecture. His rooms were well proportioned, his style elegant and restrained. He often chose soft pastel colours. His work led to the beginning of the classical revival. In London, his principal designs were the Admiralty Screen, Lansdowne House, Mansfield Street, St James's Square, Apsley House, and parts of Fitzroy Square. His most notable interiors are those of Kenwood House and Syon House. There is a large collection of his drawings in the Sir John Soane Museum.

**Barry, Sir Charles** (1795–1860) initiated the Italian palazzo style for London clubs with his designs for the Reform Club and the Travellers' Club. He designed the layout for Trafalgar Square, and was the architect for the Houses of Parliament. This design, with its classical proportions and medieval detail (executed by Pugin) show the combination of his two styles. Barry was also a brilliant landscape gardener.

**Burton, Decimus** (1800–81), the son of a builder, became a protégé of John Nash and is known as an architect of the classical revival. His work in Regent's Park includes several of the Zoo buildings and gardens, and Cornwall Terrace. He designed the Ionic screen entrance to Hyde Park, the Athenaeum Club, the former Charing Cross Hospital, and several neo-Gothic churches.

**Dance, George,** the Elder ( ?1700–68) was an architect who became Clerk of the City Works, London, in 1735. His official commissions included the Mansion House, St Leonard's Church, Shoreditch, St Matthew's, Bethnal Green and St Botolph's, Aldgate.

**Dance, George,** the Younger (1741–1825) succeeded his father as architect to the City of London in 1768 after studying in Italy. He rebuilt Newgate Prison, and this was regarded as his masterpiece. He also designed St Luke's Hospital, Old Street, All Hallows Church, London Wall, and the south front of the Guildhall. Dance was professor of architecture at the Royal Academy.

Adam: the library, Kenwood House

**Hawksmoor, Nicholas** (1661–1736) worked with Sir Christopher Wren and Sir John Vanbrugh, first as pupil and later assistant. He became Assistant Surveyor at the building of Greenwich Hospital, worked with Wren on St Paul's Cathedral and added the towers to Westminster Abbey. He designed six London churches of outstanding quality, among them St Mary Woolnoth, St Anne's Limehouse, and St George's Bloomsbury. Hawksmoor was an original, even eccentric designer, creating many exciting and dramatic effects.

**Jones, Inigo** (1573–1652) was a London-born architect who first became known as a designer of scenery and costumes for court masques. In 1615, after travel and study abroad, he became Surveyor of Works to James I, and received many official commissions, among them the Queen's House, Greenwich; the Banqueting House, Whitehall; the Queen's Chapel of St James; St Paul's Church, Covent Garden, and the nearby houses surrounding a central square, which was the first square in London. It was called Covent Garden. His loyalty to the Stuart cause brought his career to an end when the Civil War broke out. Jones, sometimes called the 'English Palladio', developed the style of the Italian Renaissance, though he adapted Italian ideas to English needs.

Most later architects, including Wren, regarded themselves as disciples of Inigo Jones.

**Kent, William** (1685–1748) was apprenticed to a coach-maker in Hull. He gave up this trade and under the patronage of Lord Burlington he achieved fame as architect, painter and designer. He designed and decorated rooms in Kensington Palace, undertook mural decorations at Hampton Court, built the Horse Guards, the Royal Mews, and the Treasury building in Whitehall. Kent was also a pioneer of English landscape gardening and was responsible for the gardens at Chiswick House. He designed the State Barge that is now in the Victoria and Albert Museum.

**Nash, John** (1752–1835), one of the leading figures of the 'picturesque' movement, was a member of the circle surrounding the Prince of Wales, later George IV. In 1806 he began work on the most extensive exercise in town planning ever carried out in London— the linking of Regent's Park to Carlton House Terrace by Portland Place, Regent Street and Lower Regent Street. He became Surveyor-General in 1813 and personal architect to the Prince Regent.

Nash's other works in London include Clarence House, the Haymarket Theatre, the United Services Club, All Souls' Church, Langham Place and Buck-

(*right*) Nash:
Cumberland
Terrace,
Regents
Park

(*below*)
Inigo Jones:
Banqueting
House,
Whitehall

ingham Palace, which was much altered at a later date. He also remodelled St James's Park. Nash was responsible for the extensive use of stucco on buildings.

**Scott, Sir George Gilbert** (1811–78) was the most prominent architect of mid-Victorian times. From 1849 onwards he was responsible for the restoration work at Westminster Abbey, St Michael's Church, Cornhill and St Margaret, Westminster. He designed the Albert Memorial, the Commonwealth Office, Foreign Office and Home Office, and also St Pancras Station Hotel. Scott 'restored' several medieval cathedrals, and was severely criticized by William Morris for his drastic methods.

**Smirke, Sir Robert** (1781–1867) was trained by Sir John Soane, and in his time altered, completed or remodelled many houses and public buildings in London, including the Royal Mint, King's College, London (an extension of Somerset House), the Library and Hall of the Inner Temple, and Covent Garden Theatre; but he is best known for the main front of the British Museum. Smirke's style is dignified and neo-classical.

**Smirke, Sidney** (1798–1877) was the younger brother of Sir Robert Smirke, and is known chiefly for the domed Reading Room of the British Museum.

**Soane, Sir John** (1753–1837) was the son of a bricklayer. In 1788 he was appointed architect to the Bank of England, which he rebuilt in 1788–1833, though only the girding wall survives. He was professor of architecture at the Royal Academy from 1806–37. He designed Dulwich College Picture Gallery, Holy Trinity Church, Marylebone Road, and the mausoleum for his wife which is in the burial ground of St Giles's Church, St Pancras. Soane left his house, now known as the Sir John Soane Museum, to the nation, together with all his furniture, antiques and paintings, with a stipulation that the collection should not be added to, and that entrance to the house should be free.

**Wren, Sir Christopher** (1632–1723) was uniquely a man of his time. He was the son of a Wiltshire parson and was educated at Westminster School and Wadham College, Oxford. His earlier interests were science, mathematics and astronomy, and his mathematical skill was of great importance when he turned his abilities towards architecture which, as befits a true Renaissance man, remained only one of his many interests. One of his first commissions was to assist with the plans for shoring-up and restoring Old St Paul's Cathedral which had fallen into disrepair under the Puritans. Then in 1666 came the Great Fire of London, and the consequent devastation stimulated Wren to produce a plan for the entire rebuilding of the City of London. This never came into being, and one

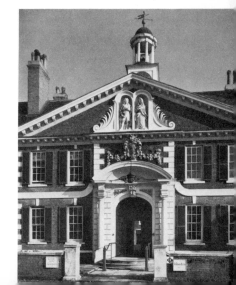

Wren: main entrance of Morden College, Blackheath

can only speculate on the beauty and splendour of Wren's London had it done so. In fact, his first major task was the rebuilding of 52 City churches and the creation of a new St Paul's.

Wren's classicism and rejection of Gothic resulted in an English Baroque style that was full of purity. St Paul's, built between 1675 and 1711, is his ecclesiastical masterpiece, but each of his smaller City churches can be called a minor masterpiece. Of the Wren churches that survived until the 20th century, many were severely damaged and some totally destroyed during the Second World War, but several of these have been brilliantly and lovingly restored.

Wren's secular buildings, beyond the limits of the City of London, include Chelsea Royal Hospital, Morden College in Blackheath, the Royal Naval College at Greenwich, the Royal Observatory at Greenwich, and Kensington Palace. The entrance to the Temple in Fleet Street was designed by Wren, as was Temple Bar, now in Theobalds Park, Hertfordshire, and the Monument, in collaboration with Robert Hooke. Marlborough House was another of his works, though extra storeys were added later. At Hampton Court Palace Wren was responsible for a new wing, the colonnade in the Clock Court, the Orangery, Fountain Court and the Garden Fronts.

---

The **Bank of England**, sometimes known as the 'Old Lady of Threadneedle Street', covers about three acres on an island site between Lothbury, Bartholomew Lane, Threadneedle Street and Princes Street, EC2. It was founded in 1694 to finance the French wars and operated in Grocers' Hall, but moved to a building on the present site in 1734. New wings were added later. Between 1788 and 1833 the building was remodelled and extended by Sir John Soane, who was responsible for the Corinthian columns and the win-

(*above*)
Bank of
England

(*right*)
Interior of
Banqueting
House:
Rubens'
ceiling

dowless walls which give the Bank the appearance of a fortress. A superstructure—a seven-storey building inside the Soane walls—was added by Sir Herbert Baker between 1925 and 1939.

**Bankside**, Southwark, SE1, runs close to the river by Hopton Street, which contains several 18th-century buildings, including the Hopton Almshouses of 1752, and Park Street, where there is a plaque marking the site of the Globe Theatre. Bankside is now lined with warehouses and dominated by a power station, but a few 17th- and 18th-century houses have survived. The *Anchor Inn* had Doctor Johnson as its manager for a year. No. 49 Park Street is reputed to be the house in which Sir Christopher Wren lodged while St Paul's was being built.

Opposite the *Anchor Inn* is a board which tells the story of the Clink Prison, first built in the 16th century, but burnt down during riots in 1780. Bankside, for many centuries, was out of the jurisdiction of the City Sheriffs, and was an area of brothels, bear- and bull-baiting arenas and theatres.

**Banqueting House**, opposite the Horse Guards in Whitehall, SW1, is all that remains of Whitehall Palace, which was destroyed by fire in 1698. Inigo Jones designed it for James I and it was completed in 1622, the first London building in the Italian tradition. Rubens decorated the ceiling with nine allegorical paintings to represent the apotheosis of James I, and his work earned him a knighthood and £3,000 from Charles I. At the north-west corner of the hall Charles I was beheaded in 1649. The lead bust of the king above the entrance was made about 1800.

Banqueting House is now used for official receptions, but is open to the public when not in use.

The **Barbican**, EC1, historically, was a fortified tower guarding the old walled City, which gave its name to the highway along which Queen Elizabeth I travelled to her coronation.    Today it is the name of a vast urban development, the purpose of which is to create a residential and recreational area covering 32 acres in the heart of the City.    Work began in 1959 on a site which was part of the largest area of war destruction in the City.

The church of St Giles, Cripplegate, stands sentinel for old London in the midst of the new.    The churchyard has been paved over and many of the headstones are set in glazed brick platforms.    Eventually a lake with fountains will be made to the north of the church. South of St Giles is part of the City wall and the semicircular remains of a bastion.

Unique in both scope and design is the Barbican Arts Centre, begun in 1971 and due to be completed in 1977.    The foundation stone was laid by Queen Elizabeth II in November 1972.    The theatre will be occupied by the Royal Shakespeare Company; the London

Tower block,
Barbican

Symphony Orchestra will find a home in the concert hall, which will also be used for conferences. There will be a cinema/lecture hall, a building for the Guildhall School of Music and Drama, a lending library, an art gallery and open-air sculpture court, restaurants, shops and a conservatory. Near by will be the new Museum of London. When it is completed the Barbican will have cost £62,000,000.

**Battersea Park** stretches from Chelsea Bridge to Albert Bridge and was formerly known as Battersea Fields, on which cabbages and asparagus were grown. It was also a duelling ground, and the scene of an encounter between the Duke of Wellington and Lord Winchelsea in 1829. In the 1850s it was laid out as a park and the swampy ground was filled with soil excavated from the Royal Victoria Dock.

For the Festival of Britain in 1951, John Piper and Osbert Lancaster designed the Festival Gardens in the north-east corner on the lines of the Tivoli Gardens in Copenhagen, and the park now has a fine river frontage. There are boating and fishing lakes, a tree walk, theatre, concert pavilion, restaurants, playing fields and a Children's Zoo. At night the gardens are brilliantly lit. The Fun Fair, also originally part of the Festival of Britain, still operates.

**Belfast (H.M.S.)** is the largest and most powerful cruiser ever built for the Royal Navy. Now a permanent Royal Naval Museum, it is moored in the Pool of London on the south bank of the Thames, opposite the Tower of London.

**Big Ben** is the bell in the 320-foot high clock tower built in 1857 at one end of the Houses of Parliament. It stands on almost the same site as the clock tower of the old palace. The bell, after an initial failure, was recast at the Whitechapel Foundry in 1858, and was called Big Ben after Sir Benjamin Hall, the First Commissioner of Works, and a Welshman of vast girth. The first day of its service as a striking clock was 11th July 1859. The clock tower was damaged in the bombing of 1941, but Big Ben continued defiantly to strike the hours. It made its first broadcast on New Year's Eve, 1923. A light above the clock is kept burning when Parliament is sitting late.

**Birdcage Walk**, on the south side of St James's Park, connects Buckingham Gate with Storey's Gate. Its name comes from the aviary that James I established there. The steps known as Cockpit Steps, at the Storey's Gate end, led from Dartmouth Street to the Cockpit, which was abolished in 1816, though cockfighting had ceased long before then.

**Blackheath Common** is a flat stretch of open space, once known as Bleak Heath, which covers an area of 267 acres. It is known that the Danes established a camp there in 1011. In 1381 Wat Tyler used it as the headquarters of his Kentish men, and in 1450 Jack Cade gathered his army on the common preparatory to marching on London. It was there that Henry VII defeated Lord Audley's Cornish rebels in 1497. When highwaymen roamed the countryside, Blackheath was a good place to avoid.

**Bloomsbury**, which takes its name from Blemund, who owned the land in the reign of King John, began its existence in the late 17th century, and development continued through the 18th century to the early 19th. Terraced houses surrounded central piazzas which later were turned into gardens shady with trees. The area quickly became fashionable, and wealthy and aristocratic families moved in. Bloomsbury Square dates from about 1660, and is one of the oldest squares in London.

Though the squares retain traces, to a greater or lesser extent, of Bloomsbury's former dignified and solid character, the old Bloomsbury is dead, mutilated by town planners and London University, whose central home it is, and whose tentacles are soon to destroy much of what is left of grace and elegance.

**Bond Street** forms the eastern boundary of Mayfair, w1. New Bond Street starts from Oxford Street and Old Bond Street from Piccadilly. Sir Thomas Bond, Comptroller of the Household to the Queen Mother, Henrietta-Maria, wife of Charles I, planned Old Bond Street in 1686. Until then it had been an open field. New Bond Street was not built until early in the 18th century. Bond Street no longer has any architectural distinction, but is a fashionable and expensive shopping street specializing in clothes, jewellery and picture-dealers' galleries. The Time-Life building, at the corner of New Bond Street and Bruton Street, has abstract carvings by Henry Moore on the balustrade.

## BRIDGES

There are 18 road and 9 railway bridges between Teddington and the sea. The following are among the most interesting or important:

**Albert Bridge,** designed by R. M. Ordish, and opened in 1873, is a combination of the cantilever and suspension principles.

**Battersea Bridge** was built in 1890 and crosses the Thames at the end of Beaufort Street. The present iron structure replaced a wooden bridge that Whistler and other artists used as a subject for their paintings, but which became unsafe and had to be closed to traffic.

**Blackfriars Bridge** was built in 1865–9 and crosses the river approximately at the point where the River Fleet once flowed into the Thames. The name Blackfriars comes from the black habits worn by the Dominicans or Black Friars, an order established in 1221, whose Priory backed on to the Thames.

**Chelsea Bridge** was opened in 1858 as a toll bridge. The toll was removed in 1879, though the toll-houses remained until 1935, when the bridge was closed for rebuilding. The new bridge, designed by L.C.C. architects, was opened in 1937, and is a graceful example of the suspension principle.

**Hammersmith Bridge,** originally erected in 1827, was the first bridge to be built on the suspension principle. The present bridge was opened in 1887.

**London Bridge** was for centuries the only bridge across the lower Thames. The first stone bridge was

Southern tower of Tower Bridge

completed in 1209, though it is likely that the Romans erected a bridge at or near this point. In the Middle Ages London Bridge had 19 arches and carried houses and shops, and there was a chapel in the middle, dedicated to St Thomas à Becket. On the spikes at either end of the drawbridge gate it was the custom to impale the heads of traitors.

John Rennie and his sons designed a successor to the medieval bridge in 1832. Over the years it became increasingly inadequate for traffic, and in 1968 dismantling of the bridge was begun. An elegant new one of pre-stressed concrete was completed in 1973. The old one was sold to America and now graces Lake Havasu City, Arizona.

**Tower Bridge**, Victorian Gothic style, was built between 1886 and 1894. It has two high towers 200 feet apart and is connected with either bank by single-span suspension bridges. The two bascules, or drawbridges, that form the carriageway, each weighing about 1,000 tons, can be raised hydraulically in 1½ minutes to enable large vessels to pass through. Few come so far up the river nowadays.

**Waterloo Bridge**, completed in 1945, was designed by Sir Giles Gilbert Scott and the engineers of the L.C.C. Well proportioned and good looking, it is made of steel and concrete, with five shallow arches each about 240 feet wide. It replaced John Rennie's original nine-arched bridge which was too narrow for modern transport.

**Westminster Bridge** is a graceful, flat-arched cast-iron bridge built in 1854–62 by Thomas Page, replacing the mid-18th century stone one to which Wordsworth's famous sonnet refers.

**Brixton Windmill**, Blenheim Gardens, SW2, was built in 1816, and is the nearest surviving windmill to the centre of London. Until 1850 it stood in open fields. It is owned by the G.L.C. and has been restored to its original condition.

**Broadcasting House**, at the southern end of Portland Place and at the corner of Langham Street, W1, is the massive building made of ferro-concrete faced with Portland stone that belongs to the British Broadcasting Corporation. It was built in 1930–1, and the architects attempted to retain the perspective which Nash had ended with the circular portico of All Souls' Church, but the plan failed when an extension was later added. Over the entrance is one of Eric Gill's last works, a sculpture of *Prospero and Ariel*.

**Brompton Oratory** (the Church of the London Oratory of St Philip Neri) in Brompton Road, SW3, is a large and elaborate attempt at the Italian Baroque style, opened in 1884 by Cardinal Newman, though the façade and dome were not completed until 1897. Inside there is a preponderance of marble and statuary, some of it from Siena Cathedral. The nave is 51 feet wide and is the third widest in England. The organ contains more than 4,000 pipes; the church is noted for its music.

**Buckingham Palace** is at the west end of the Mall, SW1. In the time of James I the site was a mulberry garden, planted to encourage the silk industry. In Charles II's reign Arlington House was built on the southern side. In 1703 it was demolished and a mansion of red brick was built in its place by the Duke of Buckingham. In 1762 George III bought it and lived in it. It was bestowed on Queen Charlotte by Act of Parliament in 1775 as part of her dowry, and became known as the Queen's House. Between 1824 and 1836 it was reconstructed in the Palladian style from the designs of John Nash. It was not occupied regularly by royalty until Queen Victoria came to the throne. The grounds consist of 40 acres, including a lake, and Royal Garden Parties are held there during the summer. One of James I's mulberry trees is still standing.

The charming little Queen's Gallery is open to the public and contains a changing display from the royal collection of paintings. The Royal Mews are to the south of the Palace. The Queen's horses and royal equipages are on show, and a variety of objects from the golden State Coach to Queen Victoria's garden chair. There are landaus, barouches and pony carriages. The harness room contains sleighs, presentation saddles and head-dress trappings.

When the sovereign is in residence, the Royal Standard is flown from the flagstaff. The guard on duty at the Palace is changed daily. The new guard marches from the parade ground of Wellington Barracks near by, and arrives in the forecourt at 11.30 a.m.; the ceremony lasts about 30 minutes.

**Bunhill Fields**, City Road, Finsbury, EC1, is possibly the site of a Saxon burial ground. It was certainly the repository for bones disinterred from the Charnel Chapel of Old St Paul's in 1547, and it is possibly then that it was given the name 'Bone-hill Fields'. It was the burial place of more than 120,000 bodies from 1665 to 1852, including thousands of victims of the Plague of London. In 1867 an Act of Parliament decreed that it should be an open space for all time in the care of the City Corporation.

Famous people buried there include William Blake, John Bunyan, Daniel Defoe, Isaac Watts, the hymn-writer, and Susannah Wesley, mother of John and Charles. Quakers were buried in a separate part of Bunhill Fields, now a recreation ground, in Roscoe Street. A small stone marks George Fox's grave.

(*above*)
Buckingham
Palace

(*right*)
Burlington
Arcade

**Burlington Arcade**, W1, links Burlington Gardens with Piccadilly. It is a covered shopping promenade in Regency style (though its façade is 1931) in the heart of the West End, and has its own beadle in attendance. Running down the arcade is forbidden, and no perambulators are allowed. Burlington Arcade was built by Samuel Ware in 1818 for Lord George Cavendish. Fashionable jewellers, hosiers and boot-makers have their shops there.

**Burlington House**, W1, on the north side of Piccadilly, was built for the first Earl of Burlington in 1665, and remodelled in 1717. The Government bought the property in 1854, and between 1868 and 1874 new wings were added, so that the 18th-century palace now has a Victorian-Renaissance façade. One of the new wings, New Burlington House, is the home of a number of learned societies, among them the Royal Society, the Geological Society, the Society of Antiquaries, the Royal Astronomical Society, the Linnaean Society and the British Association.

The main building is occupied by the Royal Academy of Arts, which was founded in 1769. The annual exhibitions of the Royal Academy are held at Burlington House from May to August, in addition to special exhibitions at other times of the year. A statue of Sir Joshua Reynolds, the first President of the Society, stands in the quadrangle.

The **Caledonian Market Clock Tower** is all that remains of the old Caledonian Market, first opened in 1855 as the Metropolitan Cattle Market. Until 1939 it was famous for the 2,500 pedlars' pitches 'on the stones'. The clock tower is 160 feet high and houses one of the largest turret clocks in London, with main wheels three feet in diameter and a seven-hundred-weight winding weight. Bombed in 1940, the clock was restarted in 1953.

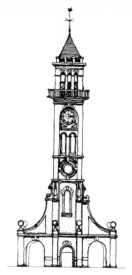

Caledonian
Market Clock
Tower

**Canals** which run through London are now practically obsolete for industrial purposes, and have been taken over by boating enthusiasts. The world they explore is silent and decayed, fascinating in its ugliness and an eerie reminder of Victorian industrialism.

The most developed area for canal-boating is between Camden Town and Paddington Basin. Boats operate from a base at Little Venice, chiefly during the summer months. British Waterways run a Waterbus to the Zoo; there is also Jason's Trip from Little Venice to Hampstead Road, and the Jenny Wren Cruise goes from Camden Town to Paddington Basin. A canal-side walk can be taken from Lisson Grove in Marylebone to the Zoo, a distance of about a mile.

**Canonbury Tower**, part of Canonbury House, in Canonbury Place, N1, was built by Prior Bolton early in the 16th century as part of a monastery, though at the Dissolution the property passed out of monastic hands. The brick tower, 66 feet high and 17 feet square, has been well preserved, and inside there are some beautiful oak-panelled rooms. Canonbury Tower has had many famous residents during its long history, among them Sir Francis Bacon, Oliver Goldsmith and Washington Irving, author of *Rip Van Winkle*.

**Carlton House Terrace**, SW1, consists of two blocks of houses designed by John Nash as residences for the aristocracy. They were the final link in the chain of Nash's work southwards from Regent's Park. The terrace was built in 1831 on what had been the garden of Carlton House, the home of George IV when he was Prince Regent. Carlton House itself, which stood on the site now marked by the Duke of York's Column, was demolished in 1828.

Carlton House Terrace

**Carlyle's House**, an early 18th-century house at 24 Cheyne Row, SW3, in Chelsea, is a fascinating literary shrine to Thomas Carlyle, who lived there from 1834 until his death in 1881. It then fell into disrepair, and was not opened as a memorial museum until 1895. The house, now National Trust property, is kept very much as it was in Carlyle's time, with letters, books and manuscripts on view, together with many personal relics.

**Carnaby Street**, a narrow shopping street in Soho, W1, has become famous as a centre for fashionably outlandish clothes. It reached its peak of popularity in the late 1960s as a rendezvous for young people, and pop music began to blare from every shop. Now it is quieter and more expensive, but is still a tourist attraction. The street is closed to traffic for most of the day.

The **Cenotaph**, Whitehall, SW1, is a memorial, made of Portland stone, to those killed in two world wars. It was designed by Sir Edwin Lutyens and unveiled on Armistice Day, 11th November 1920. Every year on Remembrance Sunday a memorial service is held at the Cenotaph, attended by the Queen, the Prime Minister, MPs and other national figures.

The **Central Criminal Court**, at the north end of Old Bailey, EC4, occupies the site of the old Newgate Prison, which was demolished in 1902. The new building, erected between 1902 and 1907, incorporates some of the stones from the prison in its lowest storey.

There had been a prison on this site since the days of King John, but it was destroyed in the Fire of London. The Gordon rioters burned down its successor in 1780, and it did not function again as a prison until 1782. Among the prisoners at Newgate were Daniel Defoe, Jack Sheppard, Jonathan Wild, Titus Oates, William Penn and Lord George Gordon. Executions were carried out in front of the prison from 1783 to 1868,

but from then until 1901 such events were confined decently to within the walls.

The Old Bailey, as it is popularly called, is the chief criminal court for London, Middlesex, parts of Surrey, Kent and Essex, and until recently contained five courts. Extensions in 1972 provided 12 new courts. The Great Hall, which was damaged in 1941, has been restored. The dome, similar to that of St Paul's, is surmounted by a bronze-gilt statue holding a sword in one hand and the scales of justice in the other. Contrary to popular belief, the figure is not blindfolded.

**Change Alley**, on the south side of Cornhill, leading into Lombard Street, EC3, saw the beginnings of the Stock Exchange, which had its first home in Jonathan's Coffee House. Another coffee house, Garraway's, had stood in Change Alley for nearly 120 years until it was demolished in 1866. Thomas Garraway was the first man to buy and sell tea in the City of London. Commemorative plaques mark the sites of the two coffee houses, and also that of the King's Head Tavern, the first home of the Marine Society.

**Changing the Guard** For this popular piece of pageantry the Queen's Life Guard is provided by the Household Cavalry. It is changed every morning at 11 a.m., alternately by the Life Guards and the Royal Horse Guards, in the small courtyard of the Horse Guards in Whitehall, sw1. On Sundays the ceremony is at 10 a.m.

At Buckingham Palace the Queen's Guard is usually provided by the Brigade of Guards. The ceremony of Changing the Guard takes place at 11.30 a.m. and lasts about half an hour. It is not held in bad weather. Full dress is worn on all occasions and when the Queen is in London her Colour of crimson is carried. At other times the Guard carries the Regimental Colour, which is based on the Union Jack. All soldiers in the Brigade of Guards wear scarlet tunics and bearskin caps. Regiments are distinguished by the plume or absence of it on the bearskin, and by the grouping of buttons on the tunic. When the Guards Divisions are away training, one of the Line regiments provides the Guard.

1865 version of Eleanor Cross, Charing Cross

**Charing Cross,** sw1, is at the junction of Whitehall and Trafalgar Square. Until 1647 a cross stood there, erected in 1291 by Edward I to mark the last stage of the funeral procession of his wife, Queen Eleanor, from Harby, Nottinghamshire, to Westminster Abbey. In 1675 an

65

equestrian statue of Charles I by Le Sueur replaced the Eleanor Cross. An 1865 version of the cross now stands in the forecourt of Charing Cross Station, in the Strand.

Charing Cross is the official centre of London for mileage measurements.

**Charterhouse** (the name is a corruption of Chartreuse) is on the north side of Charterhouse Square, near Smithfield, EC1. A Carthusian priory was built there in 1371 on ground where between 40,000 and 50,000 victims of the Black Death had been buried. After the Dissolution of the Monasteries the ownership passed to Sir Edward North, who built a mansion on the site of the little cloisters. In 1611 the house was bought by Thomas Sutton and was turned into a hostel for 80 poor gentlemen and a free school for 40 poor boys. The indigent old gentlemen who now live in chambers in Master's Court and Washhouse Court must be either bachelors or widowers, and must have been members of a profession and also of the Anglican Church. The school was transferred to Godalming in Surrey in 1872, and the school buildings are now occupied by students from St Bartholomew's Hospital.

**Cheapside**, EC2, was, in medieval times, the principal City market, and was much wider than it is today. (O.E. *cyppan* means 'to barter'.) In addition to street trading there were processions, celebrations, executions and rioting, for the apprentices were easily roused. In Tudor times the market was famous for its goldsmiths' shops. Between Friday Street (the resort of fishmongers) and Bread Street was the *Mermaid Tavern*, and the *Mitre* stood on the corner of Bread Street.

Cheapside is still busy, but its links with the past have almost completely disappeared. Memories of the old market live on in the names of the cross streets, which indicate the positions of the stalls set up by the

Chelsea Royal Hospital, south front

(below) The dining hall, Charterhouse

traders: Wood Street, Milk Street, Bread Street, Iron-monger Lane and Honey Lane.

**Chelsea Old Church**, on the Chelsea Embankment, sw3, which contained work from the 14th, 15th and 16th centuries, was practically destroyed during the Second World War, but has been rebuilt and was rededicated in 1958. The More Chapel, which dates from 1528, fortunately escaped both bombing and restoration. The church contains chained books donated by Sir Hans Sloane (1660–1753); impressive monuments and brasses; two Renaissance capitals in the archway between the More Chapel and the chancel, which were recarved in Sir Thomas More's time; a finely carved pulpit; and the More Monument. There is a small historical museum in the tower.

**Chelsea Royal Hospital** was built by Sir Christopher Wren between 1682 and 1691 on the site of a theological college. Robert Adam added to it between 1765 and 1792, and Sir John Soane completed it. The originator of the scheme was not Nell Gwyn, as legend has it, but Sir Stephen Fox. The hospital is now the home of about 500 old and disabled soldiers, who are a picturesque sight in summer in their scarlet coats.

The central portion of the building has a Doric portico flanked by a low colonnade with coupled columns, surmounted by a small tower and cupola. The Chapel is almost as Wren left it, and contains some elaborate oak carving. In the Hall there is an equestrian portrait of Charles II, by Verrio, and a statue of the king, said to be by Grinling Gibbons, is in the middle of the Centre Court. Ranelagh Gardens, the haunt of 18th-century roisterers, demi-mondaines and other pleasure-seekers, now forms part of the hospital grounds. A small museum tells the story of the hospital and the pensioners. The Chelsea Flower Show is held in the gardens annually, in late May.

The Cheshire
Cheese

The **Cheshire Cheese**, in Wine Office Court, Fleet
Street, EC4, was rebuilt in 1667, after the Great Fire,
and its oak beams, sanded floors and wooden tables
give it an authentic atmosphere, so that it is easy to
believe that the tavern was the haunt of Samuel Johnson, Oliver Goldsmith and James Boswell. Beside
the entrance to the tavern is a list of sovereigns during
whose reigns it has flourished, and there is a much
worn doorstep now protected by an iron grille.

**Chiswick House**, Burlington Lane, W4, is a villa in
the Palladian style built for Richard Boyle, third Earl
of Burlington, between 1725 and 1730. The sym-
metry of the planning and the subtlety of its detail are
outstanding. The interiors were designed by William
Kent, as was the magnificently wooded park, which is
now public property. Some of the statues in the
gardens were brought over from Hadrian's Villa at
Tivoli, near Rome.

The house has two storeys, the upper being the
principal floor, approached through a great portico,

Portico of
Chiswick
House

near which are statues of Palladio and Inigo Jones.
Two further wings were added by James Wyatt in
1788. The marble fireplaces have panels by Ricci,
and there are paintings by Kneller and Lely. In the
18th century Chiswick House was a meeting-place for
statesmen, artists and aristocrats.

The **Citadel**, the Mall, sw1, is an extraordinary
concrete building erected by the Admiralty in 1940 as
a bomb-proof shelter. The grass growing on the top
and the creeper over the sides acted as camouflage.

## CITY CHURCHES

Before the Great Fire of London there were 97
parishes within the City walls, and 10 in the 'liberties'
(the City without the Wall, originally the suburbs),
each with its own church. The oldest were Saxon in
origin, and many had Norman remains. They were
mostly small-towered Perpendicular buildings; not

more than two or three had spires.   Of the 87 churches destroyed by the Fire, 36 were not rebuilt.

When building started, Sir Christopher Wren was appointed Surveyor-General to the King's Works, and he was responsible for rebuilding 51 of them, in addition to his task of erecting the new St Paul's.

Money was raised by a tax of 3s. on every ton of coal entering the Port of London; woodwork and furnishings were provided by parishioners, who employed local craftsmen, and by private benefactors. Wren planned for towers, spires and steeples in white Portland stone or lead to blend with the City's skyline and particularly with the new cathedral. Some of the churches were small and crammed into corners; others were fine large buildings of superb architecture and craftsmanship. In all of them the font, altar and pulpit were the predominant features, and all had clear glass windows, but otherwise the interiors were very varied and were covered by every kind of ceiling. The fittings included magnificent examples of plaster work, ironwork and wood carvings.

In the 18th century about 20 of the churches were rebuilt; Nicholas Hawksmoor and George Dance the Younger were among the later architects. But the greatest change came in the middle of the 19th century. The resident population of the City had decreased tremendously, and owing to the growth of land values and the need for more offices, many of Wren's churches were sold to business firms. Between 1782 and 1939, 26 City churches disappeared, 19 of them Wren's. In 1939 only 47 churches remained, and most of these were damaged or totally destroyed by enemy action during the Second World War. Seven of the 47 have been removed or are not to be rebuilt. The rest have been restored, while one, St Mary Aldermanbury, has been taken down and rebuilt in America as a memorial to Sir Winston Churchill and Anglo-American friendship. Thus there are now only 39 City churches.

Among the most remarkable are the following:

**All Hallows Barking-by-the-Tower**, Great Tower Street, EC1, has a history going back to Saxon times, and remains of that period were found after the church had been bombed in 1941; a tessellated pavement of about AD 45 and some pre-Conquest relics were also uncovered. With the aid of gifts from many parts of the world, the church has been rebuilt; it was rededicated in 1957. A spire was added to the tower—the first shaped spire in the City since Wren's time. The pulpit came from St Swithin's, London Stone, a church that was totally destroyed. There are some interesting brasses dating from 1389 to 1651, and a famous font cover by Grinling Gibbons which depicts cupids stealing grapes.

**All Hallows London-Wall**, London Wall, EC2, was rebuilt by George Dance the Younger in 1765. From outside it looks an uninteresting oblong with a·Portland stone tower and cupola, but the interior is light and elegant. The white and gold ceiling is barrel-vaulted and lit by the semi-circular windows of the clerestory. The north wall is part of the old City wall.

**St Andrew-by-the-Wardrobe**, Queen Victoria Street, EC4, is a Wren church (1686–93) that had its interior completely gutted in 1940; this has been entirely renewed. Its most attractive feature now is the ceiling, with quadripartite vaulting over the aisles and barrel-vaulting over the nave. Its name comes from its nearness to a building which housed the Master of the King's Wardrobe, an office abolished in 1709.

**St Andrew Holborn**, Holborn Circus, EC1, was the largest of Wren's parish churches, built in 1686–7. It was restored in 1961 after being bombed. The church is particularly interesting in that it contains Handel's beautiful 18th-century organ-case from the Foundling Hospital at Coram's fields; the gilded altar-piece and the wrought-iron altar rails also came from there. The church contains the tomb of Thomas Coram, who founded the Hospital, and who rescued his first foundling from the steps of St Andrew's. In the north wall is one of the two remaining resurrection stones in the City.

**St Andrew Undershaft**, a pre-Great Fire church in Leadenhall Street, EC3, is built in a stately Gothic style. The interior, rebuilt in 1520–32, has north and south aisle arcades of six bays. The fine west window is of 17th-century glass and shows English monarchs and heraldry. Nicholas Stone designed the font, and also the marble and alabaster monument to John Stow, the first historian of London. The quill pen in his hand is renewed annually by the Lord Mayor on or near 5th April, the anniversary of Stow's death.

**St Bartholomew-the-Great**, West Smithfield, EC1, is a relic of the Augustinian Priory and Hospital that was built by Rahere, a member of the courts of William Rufus and Henry I, about 1123. He later became a monk.

After the Dissolution, most of the priory buildings were pulled down and the site of the nave became a churchyard. Only the east end remained. The dilapidated church was repaired early in the 17th century, when a new brick tower was built. In the tower are five medieval bells, the oldest complete ring in London. Later, the church was used for various secular purposes. Restoration was carried out by Sir Aston Webb in the 1890s.

Among the fine monuments in the church the most outstanding is the effigy of Prior Rahere on his tomb, lying to the north of the sanctuary. A 16th-century canopy surmounts it. The font is the only pre-Reformation font in the City.

**St Benet, Paul's Wharf** (also known as St Benet's

Welsh Church), Upper Thames Street, EC4, is a Wren church, rather Dutch in character on account of its red and blue brickwork. The north and west galleries, between Corinthian columns, are original, as are the old stone floors; the pews are made from the wood of the original box pews.

**St Botolph, Aldersgate**, Aldersgate Street, EC1, was a medieval church rebuilt either in 1754 or in 1788–91 by Nathaniel Wright. The tower and wooden bell turret with its gilded vane are attractive. The late 18th-century interior contains elaborate plaster work which decorates the barrel-vaulted roof. Over the north and south aisles wooden galleries are supported by panelled columns. The east window is the only 18th-century transparency in the City.

**St Bride, Fleet Street**, off Fleet Street, EC4, is the church of journalists and printers. Dating from the 12th century, it was rebuilt by Wren after its destruction in the Great Fire. The steeple has been described as a 'madrigal in stone'. In 1940 St Bride's was gutted during a heavy air raid; it was later restored by Godfrey Allen, who made use of Wren's original drawings. One good result of the bombing was the evidence that was found dating the church many centuries earlier than had been thought. Roman remains were discovered, and stone from the first 6th-century church. There were also several thousand human bones laid in chequer-board pattern. In the crypt is a fascinating exhibition of the church's history, with the new archaeological finds on view.

**St Dunstan-in-the-West**, Fleet Street, EC4, was rebuilt on an unusual octagonal plan by John Shaw in 1831, and completed after his death by his son. Its tower dominates Fleet Street, and the eight bells, which came from the older church, were those of Dickens's story, *The Chimes*. William Tyndale, translator of the New Testament, preached there, as

St Michael,
Paternoster Royal

St
Dunstan-
in-the-
West, Fleet
Street

did the poet and mystic John Donne, Dean of St Paul's. Izaak Walton was a member of the congregation, and a vestryman from 1629–44.

The fine clock, dating from 1671, has two giant wooden figures which strike the hours and quarters, and turn their heads. It belonged to the old church and was returned from St Dunstan's, Regent's Park, where it had been since 1831, by Viscount Rothermere in 1935. A bust of Lord Northcliffe, his brother, adorns the front of the church. The statue of Queen Elizabeth I over the vestry door dates from 1586 (later restored) and came from the Lud Gate which stood halfway up Ludgate Hill until 1760.

**St Ethelburga, Bishopsgate**, Bishopsgate, EC2, is a medieval church, the smallest in the City, built of ragstone and brick. It escaped the Great Fire, but there has been much alteration and restoration since. It consists of a nave and south aisle only, separated by a 15th-century arcade.

**St Giles, Cripplegate**, Fore Street, EC2. The interior has been extensively restored after bombing, though the 15th-century arcade of seven bays remains, together with the stone corbels and some stone arches in the sanctuary. The burial place of John Milton is marked on a stone at the threshold of the chancel. In the churchyard are fragments of the medieval London Wall. The church is in the Barbican development.

**St Helen, Bishopsgate**, off Bishopsgate, EC2, is another medieval church which escaped the Great Fire. Inside, there are flat timber roofs over two aisles of equal width, one originally belonging to a Benedictine nunnery. Because it has so many monuments, St Helen's has been called the 'Westminster Abbey of the City'.

**St James, Garlickhythe**, Garlick Hill, EC4, is a Wren church that was bombed, but has been most

St Mary-le-Bow

St Bride,
Fleet Street

St Magnus
the Martyr

skilfully restored. The tower, of rough stone, has a graceful early 18th-century steeple of Portland stone. The interior is higher than that of any other City church. There are round-headed windows of clear glass and the roof is clerestoried; thus a great deal of light is allowed in, and the vaulted ceiling with its gilded plaster work benefits greatly. Ironwork and carved wood are plentiful; there are hat pegs in the churchwardens' pews and a wig stand on the pulpit.

**St Katharine Creechurch** (a corruption of Christchurch), Leadenhall Street, EC3, was rebuilt in 1628–31 (a rare period for church building in England) in the Renaissance style, though the squat tower (1504) belongs to an earlier church. The pretty wooden turret redeems its plainness. There is much beauty inside, with the classical free-standing columns, Tudor clerestory and vaulting, the white walls with mouldings picked out in grey and bosses brightly painted. There is some richly carved woodwork and several handsome monuments.

**St Lawrence Jewry**, Gresham Street, EC2, is a magnificent Wren church next to the Guildhall which was completely gutted during the blitz and restored in such a way that the splendour of a Corporation Church has not been diminished. The Royal Arms and those of the City of London retain their sombre dignity. All the fittings are new. The furniture is of dark polished wood, and there is a lot of gold about, given by the City Corporation. Fortunately, the tower and walls remain Wren's, and the steeple is a faithful copy of his work.

**St Magnus the Martyr**, Lower Thames Street, EC3, has a history going back over 1,000 years. It was built of stone, showing its important position right beside the Thames crossing. A later church stood at the head of old London Bridge, the footway to which passed under the tower after the houses on the bridge were demolished in 1760. The church was rebuilt to Wren's design after the Great Fire, and when the old bridge was replaced by the present one, which is some yards further west, the church lost its near neighbour. St Magnus's small churchyard is part of the old road of London Bridge.

The sturdy tower is of Portland stone and is one of the three finest Wren towers in the City; the steeple is one of his most complex erections. The projecting clock was given in 1709 by Charles Duncombe, Lord Mayor at the time.

Inside, the church is magnificently furnished. It is renowned for its wealth of richly carved woodwork and wrought-iron ware, nearly all contemporary with Wren's building.

**St Margaret, Lothbury**, Lothbury, EC2, is a restored Wren church of white Portland stone; it has a lead steeple. The interior woodwork is dark and elaborately carved, contrasting well with the white and gold walls and the brass candelabra. The marble font is carved with scriptural subjects in relief, reputedly by Grinling Gibbons.

**St Margaret Pattens**, Eastcheap, EC3, is a Wren church with a tower of Portland stone; its lead medieval-type spire is 200 feet high and is one of Wren's best. The dark old woodwork, grey columns with gilded capitals and white walls give a pleasant effect. The 18th-century monuments and the cherubs on the marble font are attractive additions to the harmony.

**St Martin, Ludgate**, Ludgate Hill, EC4, is one of Wren's later churches. The south front is of Portland stone; the dark spire enhances the dome of St Paul's as seen from Fleet Street. Inside, a notable feature is a screen with carved door-cases and a gallery above, and there is much 17th-century work.

**St Mary Abchurch**, Cannon Street, EC4, was designed by Wren in pale red brick with stone dressings and has a most delicate lead spire. Its painted dome, which rests on eight arches supported by massive walls, is its chief attraction, but there is also much splendid woodwork, together with 18th-century monuments and urns, and a fine altar-piece by Grinling Gibbons.

**St Mary Aldermary**, Queen Victoria Street, EC2, stands prominently at the traffic intersection by Mansion House Station. It was rebuilt by Wren after the Great Fire; the interior suffered in the blitz. It is in

Gothic style throughout, and is often said to be the earliest Gothic revival building in England.

**St Mary-at-Hill**, Eastcheap, EC3, was rebuilt by Wren in 1676, though the tower was not erected until 1788. It has probably the most beautiful interior of any of the City churches. The square-domed centre rests on Corinthian columns. The woodwork is massive, but the effect is lightened by the delicate Adam-like plaster work. The west end has a screen of glass and wood, a gallery and organ-case. The pulpit is approached by a wooden staircase with carved balusters, the high box-pews have elegant sword-rests, and the windows are of clear glass with a few bands of colour.

**St Mary-le-Bow**, Cheapside, EC2, has a special place in the hearts of Londoners for it is said that only those who were born within the sound of its bells are true Cockneys. The bells were installed in the 15th and 16th centuries to guide travellers to the City of London, and to signal the end of the working day. The name is derived from the bows or arches of the early Norman crypt, which has three aisles with cushion capitals. The church was rebuilt by Wren in 1670–83. In 1941 it was extensively damaged and the original bells were lost. After the war the steeple was taken down so that the tower could be strengthened and then re-erected, stone by stone. The new bells were first rung by the Duke of Edinburgh in 1961.

**St Mary Woolnoth**, Lombard Street, EC3, is a medieval church which survived the Great Fire but had to be demolished in 1716. Nicholas Hawksmoor designed the new church in 1716–27. The unusual tower divides at the top into two small turrets. The west front has a fine entrance and the north side has some elaborate niches. Inside, four great semi-circular-headed windows give plenty of light and show up the plaster ceiling. The carved altar-piece is very

St Vedast,
Foster Lane

St Mary
Woolnoth:
interior

Baroque, and the inlaid pulpit and sounding-board are typically Hawksmoor.

**St Michael, Paternoster Royal**, College Hill, EC4, derives its name from the former nearby Paternoster Lane, and the connection that the neighbouring Vintry Ward had with the wine town of La Reole, near Bordeaux. It is known as Whittington's Church, for it was Sir Richard Whittington who was responsible for rebuilding the 13th-century church. He died in 1423 and was buried on the north side of the high altar, but his tomb was destroyed with the church in the Great Fire.

The church was one of the last to be rebuilt to Wren's designs. It was reconstructed between 1686 and 1694, and is in red brick with Portland stone facings and dressings. The tower was not completed until 1713. In 1944 a flying-bomb crashed through the roof and wrecked the interior. The church was restored and rededicated in 1968 as the Headquarters of the Missions to Seamen.

The pulpit is by Grinling Gibbons, the 17th-century candelabra came from All Hallows-the-Great, and there are some strikingly dramatic modern stained glass windows, one of them depicting Dick Whittington and his cat.

**St Olave, Hart Street**, Fenchurch Street, EC3, escaped the Great Fire but was almost totally destroyed during the Second World War. After restoration in 1951-4, King Haakon of Norway laid the 'King's Stone' before the sanctuary in memory of Olaf, King of Norway, to whom the church is dedicated, and who was martyred in 1030. Samuel Pepys is closely associated with St Olave's and worshipped in the 15th-century building. There is a memorial to Pepys, who is buried in the church, and a monument erected for his wife, for which he wrote the Latin inscription. The gate into the churchyard is surmounted by spikes, skulls and crossbones.

**St Peter Cornhill**, Cornhill, EC3, is a restored Wren church with Victorian pews and windows above the altar-piece. It has a large amount of carved wood-work, white walls, pulpit and sounding-board, and a marble font with carved wooden cover. The screen is one of the only two in a Wren church. The dark red brick tower is surmounted with a green copper dome, and on top of the spire are St Peter's keys in gold.

**St Sepulchre-without-Newgate** (the Church of the Holy Sepulchre), Holborn Viaduct, opposite the Old Bailey, is the largest church in the City. It survived the Great Fire but has been much altered over the years. The vaulted plaster ceiling of 1830 is note-worthy, so is the organ-case decorated with gilded cherubs and carrying the pea-pod device of Grinling Gibbons; the octagonal font cover is also bedecked with cherubs.

In a glass case is a hand-bell with which watchmen of St Sepulchre's roused condemned prisoners of New-gate Prison on the eve of their execution.

**St Stephen Walbrook**, Walbrook, EC4, is one of Wren's masterpieces, a purely Baroque conception, and it has been beautifully restored. The dome, which Wren designed before he did that of St Paul's, with eight arches supported by 16 Corinthian pillars, is lit by oval windows, round-headed west windows and a clerestory. Many of the fittings are contemporary, including the pulpit, the altar-rails, altar-piece and font; unfortunately the pews have gone. The whole effect is of light, space and order.

**St Vedast, Foster Lane**, Cheapside, EC2, is a Wren church built on medieval remains; owing to bombing, it has had to be drastically restored. The spire of the white stone tower appears to be simple, but in fact it is one of Wren's most subtle in the way that concave yields to convex; it is topped by an obelisk and vane.

Inside, the impression is of a college chapel, with facing seats. The flat ceiling is beautifully and elaborately decorated with wreaths of leaves and flowers. Attached to the north side of the church is Wren's charming cloister, with tiny rooms over it, which escaped the havoc of 1940.

Sphinx at base of Cleopatra's Needle

**Cleopatra's Needle**, Victoria Embankment, WC2, is not a needle and has only the slenderest connection with Cleopatra. It is an obelisk of pink granite, 68½ feet high, weighing more than 180 tons. It is one of two erected at Heliopolis by Thotmes III *c.* 1500 BC. They were later removed to Alexandria by the Emperor Augustus and, as Cleopatra had died there a few years before, they became associated with her.

The obelisk was offered to Britain by Mehemet Ali in 1819, but was declined. It was not until 1877 that it left Alexandria and began an eventful voyage, during which six sailors lost their lives in stormy seas. It was erected on its present site in 1878; in 1881 its companion was put up in New York's Central Park.

The base of the obelisk still has scars inflicted by bombs in 1917. Inscriptions on the pedestal relate to its history.

**Clerks' Well**, from which the district of Clerkenwell got its name, lies at the bottom of some steep steps behind a small locked door between Nos. 14 and 18 Farringdon Road, EC1. It was the well of the parish clerks, the men who were in day to day charge of the parish churches, and was mentioned by William Fitz-stephen in his biography of Thomas à Becket, and by John Stow in his *Survey of London*. The clerks used to assemble at the well every year and perform Mystery Plays.

In 1800 a pump to bring water up from the well was fixed to the wall outside. Above the spout of the pump was an iron plate on which was written a short account of the well. The well was closed in 1857, and its existence was forgotten until 1924, when excavations on an adjoining site were being made.

**Cock Lane**, EC1, at its junction with Giltspur Street, was once known as Pie Corner, the northernmost spot reached by the Great Fire of 1666, according to legend. High on the wall of the corner house is the naked figure of a plump golden boy on a pedestal. The figure, formerly outside the *Fortunes of War* Tavern, represents Greed. The fire, said the preachers, was God's judgement on the gluttony of the people of London. There is little doubt, however, that Pie Corner got its name from the Court of Pie Powder, a corruption of *pied poudreux* (dusty-footed), a court of summary jurisdiction held in connection with medieval fairs.

The **College of Arms** (also known, but incorrectly, as the College of Heralds) in Queen Victoria Street, EC4, is the seat of the official heraldic authority for the United Kingdom. Incorporated by Richard III in 1484, it operated from Derby House, on the site of which stands the present building. Derby House was destroyed in the Great Fire, and a new College, of pleasant red brick, was built between 1672 and 1688. The splendid 19th-century wrought-iron gates were set up in 1956.

The College of Arms establishes coats of arms and undertakes genealogical research. The collections of heraldic and genealogical records are unique.

## COMMEMORATIVE PLAQUES ───────────

One of the minor pleasures of wandering around London is to come across the blue plaques placed on houses of historical interest. Famous Londoners and visitors to London from all professions and walks of life have been honoured in this way, and the plaques, in their modest way, provide an instant sense of history.

The conditions for putting up a plaque are strict. The subject must have been held in high regard by his or her peers, must have made an important contribution to human welfare or happiness, and his name and fame must have survived into the next generation. People are not usually considered until 20 years after their death. A foreigner must have had an international reputation or considerable eminence in his own country, and his stay in London must have been of significance in his life's work. Foreigners are not normally considered until 50 years after their death. There are well over 300 plaques to be seen in London. The following is a representative selection:

**Adam, Robert** (1728–92) Architect.  1–3 Robert Street, Adelphi, WC2.
**Arnold, Matthew** (1822–88) Poet.  2 Chester Square, SW1.
**Baird, John Logie** (1888–1946) 22 Frith Street, W1. Baird first demonstrated television in this house in 1926.
**Barrie, Sir James Matthew** (1860–1937) Author and dramatist. Creator of *Peter Pan*.  100 Bayswater Road, W2.
**Beardsley, Aubrey** (1872–98) Artist.  114 Cambridge Street, SW1.
**Beerbohm, Sir Max** (1872–1956) Author and artist.  57 Palace Gardens Terrace, W8.
**Bennett, Arnold** (1867–1931) Novelist and dramatist.  75 Cadogan Square, SW1.
**Berlioz, Hector** (1803–69) French composer.  58 Queen Anne Street, W1. One of Berlioz's visits to London was expressly to judge musical instruments at the Great Exhibition of 1851.
**Boswell, James** (1740–95) Diarist and biographer, notably of Dr Johnson.  122 Great Portland Street, W1.
**Browning, Elizabeth Barrett** (1806–61) Poet.  99 Gloucester Place, W1. Also 50 Wimpole Street, W1. The plaque marks the site of the house, now demolished.

College of
Arms, Queen
Victoria
Street

(*below*)
Georgian
Colonnade,
Coram's
Fields

**Brunel, Sir Marc Isambard** (1769–1849) and **Brunel, Isambard Kingdom** (1806–59) Civil engineers. 98 Cheyne Walk, sw10.

**Chippendale, Thomas** (c. 1718–79) Cabinet-maker. The site of his workshop was at 61 St Martin's Lane, wc2.

**Constable, John** (1776–1837) Landscape painter. 40 Well Walk, nw3.

**Dickens, Charles** (1812–70) Novelist. 48 Doughty Street, wc1.

**Dryden, John** (1631–1700) Poet and dramatist. 43 Gerrard Street, w1.

**'Eliot, George'** (Mary Ann Cross) (1819–80) Holly Lodge, Wimbledon Park Road, sw19. Also 4 Cheyne Walk, sw10.

**Freud, Sigmund** (1859–1939) German founder of psycho-analysis. 20 Maresfield Gardens, nw3.

**Galsworthy, John** (1867–1933) Novelist and dramatist. Grove Lodge, Hampstead Grove, nw3.

**Gaskell, Mrs Elizabeth Cleghorn** (1810–65) Novelist. 93 Cheyne Walk, sw10.

**Grahame, Kenneth** (1859–1932) Author of *The Wind in the Willows*. 16 Phillimore Place, w8.

**Handel, George Frederick** (1685–1759) English composer of German birth. 25 Brook Street, w1.

**Hardy, Thomas** (1840–1928) Poet and novelist. 172 Trinity Road, sw17.

**Hawthorne, Nathaniel** (1804–64) American author. 4 Pond Road, se3.

**Irving, Sir Henry** (1838–1905) Actor. 15a Grafton Street, w1.

**Kipling, Rudyard** (1865–1936) Poet and writer. 43 Villiers Street, wc2.

**Lamb, Charles** ('Elia') (1775–1834) Essayist. 64 Duncan Terrace, n1.

**Lear, Edward** (1812–88) Artist and nonsense poet. 30 Seymour Street, w1.

**Marconi, Guglielmo** (1874–1937) Italian-born pioneer of wireless telegraphy. 71 Hereford Road, w2.

**Moore, George** (1852–1933) Irish-born author. 121 Ebury Street, sw1.

**Morse, Samuel** (1791–1872) American inventor of the Morse Code. 141 Cleveland Street, w1.

**Mozart, Wolfgang Amadeus** (1756–91) Austrian composer. 180 Ebury Street, sw1.

**Pepys, Samuel** (1633–1703) Secretary of the Admiralty and diarist. 12 Buckingham Street, wc2.

**Rossetti, Dante Gabriel** (1828–82) Poet and painter. 16 Cheyne Walk, sw10. **A. C. Swinburne** also lived here. There are other memorials to Rossetti at 110 Hallam Street, w1, where he was born, and at 17 Red Lion Square, wc10. At the latter address lived **William Morris** (1834–96) and **Sir Edward Burne-Jones** (1833–98).

**Rowlandson, Thomas** (1757–1827) Satirical artist. 16 John Adam Street, wc2.

**Sheraton, Thomas** (1751–1806) Furniture designer.   163 Wardour Street, w1.

**Swinburne, Algernon Charles** (1837–1909) Poet.   11 Putney Hill, sw15.

**Terry, Dame Ellen** (1847–1928) Actress.   22 Barkston Gardens, sw5.

**Thackeray, William Makepeace** (1811–63) Novelist.   16 Young Street, w8.   Also at 2 Palace Green, w8 and 36 Onslow Square, sw7.

**Thomas, Edward** (1878–1917) Poet and author.   61 Shelgate Road, sw11.

**Trollope, Anthony** (1815–82) Novelist.   39 Montague Square, w1.

**'Mark Twain' (Samuel Langhorne Clemens)** (1835–1910) American writer.   23 Tedworth Square, sw3.

**Wesley, John** (1703–91) Founder of Methodism.   47 City Road, ec1.

**Whistler, James Abbot McNeil** (1834–1903) American painter.   96 Cheyne Walk, sw10.

**Wilde, Oscar** (1854–1900) Poet and dramatist.   34 Tite Street, sw3.

---

**Congress House**, in Great Russell Street, wc1, is the headquarters of the Trades Union Congress, and was opened in 1958.   It is noteworthy for the powerful Epstein sculpture which commemorates the trade unionists killed in two wars.   Epstein carved it on the site from a solid block of Roman stone weighing 10 tons.

**Coram's Fields**, on the north side of Guilford Street, wc1, is now a children's playground flanked by Georgian colonnades.   It was formerly the site of the Foundling Hospital, founded by Thomas Coram, mariner, empire-builder and philanthropist, in 1739 for 'exposed and deserted children'.   The hospital buildings were demolished and the hospital moved to Berkhamsted in 1926.   The offices of the Foundling Hospital, now called the Thomas Coram Foundation for Children, still exist at 40 Brunswick Square, and contain interesting relics of the old building, including part of the beautiful oak staircase. The Court Room has been re-erected with much of the original woodwork, ceiling and plaster decoration. Handel was interested in Coram's work and presented the organ in the chapel; a manuscript score of *Messiah* is displayed in the picture gallery.

The **Corn Exchange**, in Mark Lane, EC3, was once an open quadrangle, three sides of which consisted of piazzas supported by pillars. Under them were 64 stalls and bins for holding grain. When the Corn Laws were repealed in 1845 business increased to such an extent that a new Corn Exchange had to be built. It was partly destroyed in 1941, and rebuilt and expanded in 1953.

**Cornhill**, a busy street lined mainly with tall office buildings, runs along the south side of the Royal Exchange into Leadenhall Street, EC3. It is the site of the Roman town hall and market-place, and in medieval times a grain market was held there. The first coffee house in London was opened in 1652 in St Michael's Alley. Beside this alley is the *George and Vulture*, known to readers of Dickens. There are two Wren churches in Cornhill, St Michael's and St Peter's, the latter traditionally the earliest Christian church in London.

**County Hall**, at the junction of Belvedere Road and the south end of Westminster Bridge, SE1, is the headquarters of the Greater London Council, and was built in 1912–22 on waste land known as 'Pedlar's Acre'. Additions were made in later years. The building is in Edwardian Renaissance style. The interior contains ancient fireplaces, one dating from *c.* 1752, which were taken from old buildings being pulled down while County Hall was being built. There is some beautiful marble work in the Council Chambers and corridors.

County Hall from Victoria Embankment

**Covent Garden Theatre**, also known as the Royal Opera House, Covent Garden, is on the north side of Covent Garden Market, wc2. There has been a theatre on the site since 1732. The present building, with its Corinthian colonnade, dates from 1858, the previous buildings having been burned in 1808 and 1856. Covent Garden Theatre specializes in lavish opera productions alternating with performances by the Royal Ballet.

**Crosby Hall**, at the corner of Danvers Street and Cheyne Walk, sw3, was originally the Great Hall of Crosby Place, a mansion built in 1466 by Sir John Crosby, and mentioned in Shakespeare's *Richard III*. The Duke of Gloucester, later Richard III, lived there; Sir Thomas More bought it in 1523. In the 17th century much of it was burned down. Fortunately the Hall escaped, but only to have a chequered career for the next 200 years, finishing up as a restaurant. In 1908 the Hall was bought by the University and City Association of London, and two years later was re-erected on its present site, which was part of Sir Thomas More's Chelsea garden. It now belongs to the British Federation of University Women. The Hall has an oak hammer-beam roof and oriel windows, both among the finest examples of their kind. The high table is Jacobean and much of the furniture is Cromwellian.

The **Custom House**, in Lower Thames Street, EC3, just beyond Billingsgate, is the headquarters of the Collector of Customs for the Port of London. It dates from 1815–7 and is the sixth building to be erected on or near this site.

The present building is a large classical edifice with a fine river façade. It contains a Library, a collection of curios appertaining to customs, and old-fashioned armed equipment. The documents required by Custom Laws are received by officials in the Long Room, which is 190 feet by 66 feet.

The **Cutty Sark**, the last survivor of the famous tea-clippers, launched in 1869, lies in a permanent berth in King William Walk, near Greenwich Pier, SE10. The name means 'short shift', as worn by the witch in Robert Burns's poem *Tam o' Shanter*; the clipper's figurehead was a witch. On board is a museum full of items of maritime interest, and in the lower hold is a fascinating collection of ships' figureheads.

The **Design Centre**, at 28 Haymarket, SW1, is the headquarters of the Council of Industrial Design, and shows changing exhibitions of a variety of British products that are considered by the Council to be well designed. Its photographic reference library, called Design Index, is particularly noteworthy, containing as it does some 10,000 photographs and samples of British products.

**Dickens House,** 48 Doughty Street, WC1, is a neat, prim little house in which Charles Dickens lived from 1837 to 1839, his first real home in London, and the only surviving one. There he completed *The Pick-*

Dr Johnson's House, Gough Square

Dickens House, Doughty Street

*wick Papers,* wrote *Oliver Twist* and *Nicholas Nickleby,* and planned *Barnaby Rudge.* The house was bought by the Dickens Fellowship and opened in 1925 as a Library and Museum. There is a fine collection of Dickensiana, including a lock of his hair, a writing table, his favourite reading desk, portraits and photographs, letters, manuscripts and first editions of his works. In the basement is a reproduction of the Dingley Dell kitchen.

**H.M.S. Discovery**, now permanently moored to Victoria Embankment and used as a training ship of the Royal Naval Volunteer Reserve, was originally built for use in scientific research in polar conditions, and was launched in 1901. Captain Scott took the ship to Antarctica the same year and returned in 1904. Scott's cabin is on view, also a small collection of his letters and personal possessions connected with his dash to the South Pole in the *Terra Nova,* in 1910. Scott took the *Discovery* on his ill-fated journey to Antarctica in 1912.

**Doctor Johnson's House**, 17 Gough Square, EC4, approached through Johnson's Court and Bolt Court, on the north side of Fleet Street, is a pleasant example of Queen Anne domestic architecture. Doctor Johnson lived there from 1748 to 1759. The house contains many Johnson relics, including letters and two first editions of the *Dictionary.* The most interesting feature is the garret at the top in which the *Dictionary* was written by Johnson and his six assistants. Many of the exhibits in the house were presented by American admirers of Johnson.

**Downing Street**, off Whitehall, SW1, was built originally by Sir George Downing, Secretary to the Treasury in the reign of Charles II, *c.* 1663–71. The north side was rebuilt in 1722 and again in 1766–74, and restored in 1960–4. No. 10, the official residence

of the Prime Minister, was conferred on Robert Walpole by George II in 1731, but he did not move there until 1735. The Chancellor of the Exchequer lives at No. 11 Downing Street, and No. 12 is the office of the Government Whip.

Remains of part of the Palace of Whitehall have been found during demolition work in Downing Street, as well as a Saxon structure and Roman and Tudor pottery.

**Drury Lane Theatre** (Theatre Royal, Drury Lane) has its main entrance in Catherine Street, WC2. The first theatre on the site was opened in 1663, and Nell Gwyn is supposed to have sold oranges in the pit before she became an actress in 1665. The theatre was rebuilt by Wren in 1674, after a fire. The present building, with a large colonnade at the side, was designed by Benjamin Wyatt in 1812. There were additions in 1831 and alterations in 1922. It is the only piece of Georgian theatre design left in London.

The **Duke of York's Column**, at the south end of Waterloo Place, SW1 (a copy of Trajan's Column in Rome), was erected in 1833 as a memorial to the Duke of York, second son of George III. It was financed by the deduction of a day's pay from every soldier in the army, from drummer-boy to general. The column is 124 feet high and is surmounted by a 14-foot high bronze statue of the Duke, who was Commander-in-Chief of the British Army from 1798 until 1827, the year of his death. The Duke is chiefly remembered nowadays for leading ten thousand men up the hill and down again. Beyond the column the Waterloo, or Duke of York's Steps, descend to St James's Park.

The **Elfin Oak**, in Kensington Gardens, was carved by Ivor Innes in 1930 from an old tree stump found in Richmond Park. Varieties of painted fairies, elves and woodland animals peep coyly out of holes and from round corners, or swarm up and down the trunk.

**Ely Place** is a private cul-de-sac off Charterhouse Street, EC1, and was the site of the medieval town palace of the bishops of Ely. It contains St Etheldreda's Church, the only pre-Reformation church in London which has been restored to the Roman Catholic authority. As late as last century the Queen's writ was not valid in Ely Place, and the inhabitants were free from taxation.

**Eros**, in the centre of Piccadilly Circus, W1, is really the Angel of Christian Charity, although it is often referred to as the Greek god of Love. The pyramidal bronze fountain surmounted by a winged figure of an archer with his bow is the Shaftesbury Memorial, designed by Alfred Gilbert. It was unveiled in 1893 in

(*above*) View down the River Thames from County Hall

PLATE 1

(*right*) Centre Point, a modern office block, and St Giles-in-the-Fields

(*above*) Roof of Henry VII's Chapel, Westminster Abbey, showing fan vaulting

PLATE 2

(*left*) The White Tower, the Norman keep of the Tower of London

PLATE 3

The South Front of Hampton Court Palace, designed by Sir Christopher Wren

Queen Charlotte's State Bedroom, Hampton Court Palace

(*above*) The statue of Physical Energy, by G. F. Watts, Kensington Gardens

PLATE 4

(*left*) The Albert Memorial, Kensington Gardens

Parliament Square, with the Houses of Parliament and St Margaret, Westminster

PLATE 5

The Commonwealth Institute

Petticoat
Lane Market
Middlesex
Street

PLATE 6

Portobello
Road Market

PLATE 7

Canonbury Tower and Canonbury House, Islington

Shepherd Market, an attractive 'village' quarter off Piccadilly

PLATE 8    Interior of St Stephen Walbrook, designed by Sir Christopher Wren

memory of the Earl of Shaftesbury, the Victorian philanthropist. The steps form a popular focal and rendezvous point for tourists, who throng its island site in the summer season.

Eros,
Piccadilly
Circus

The **Fleet River**, also known as Fleet Ditch, was always a foul stream and is now, appropriately, a sewer. It rises in the heights of Hampstead, flows through Holborn Valley ('Hole-bourne', or stream in the hollow), goes under Ludgate Circus and joins the Thames through a pipe under Blackfriars Bridge, where it can be seen at low tide. In 1737 the river was covered in as far as Ludgate Circus, and the rest disappeared in 1765, to the relief of the people who lived near it.

**Fleet Street**, which runs from Temple Bar to Ludgate Circus, is only half a mile long, but is one of the most famous streets in the world. It has been associated with printing since Wynkyn de Worde, Caxton's assistant, set up his printing press in 'Fletestrete at the signe of the Sonne' in 1500. The first daily paper printed in Fleet Street was the *Daily Courant* in 1702. Now all the great national and provincial newspapers have offices in or near Fleet Street.

Historic buildings in or just off the street include St Bride's Church, the parish church of the Press, the *Cock Tavern*, the *Cheshire Cheese*, both belonging to the 17th century, the Church of St Dunstan-in-the-West, Child's Bank, first established in the mid-17th century, and Prince Henry's Room, a Jacobean house. The entrance to the Temple is in the street, and many alleys and courts running off it have literary and historical associations. It is the principal route from the City to Westminster, the boundary being at Temple Bar, and thus has seen many regal and civic processions.

The **George Inn**, Borough High Street, Southwark, SE1, is the only remaining inn in Southwark of those which were the starting-points for regular coach services to parts of southern England. Rebuilt after a fire in 1677, it surrounded three sides of a courtyard, and the bedrooms opened straight on to the galleries, but the north and centre wings were demolished in 1889, and only the south wing survives. The property was presented to the National Trust in 1937. It is the one remaining galleried inn in London, and was mentioned in Dickens's *Little Dorrit*.

**Gibbons, Grinling** (1648–1721), a wood-carver and sculptor, was born in Rotterdam, though his father was English. After settling in England, his talent was discovered by the diarist John Evelyn. He became master carver in wood to the Crown and remained so until the time of George I. His association with Wren was a unique collaboration between architect and master craftsman. His work can be seen in several City churches, and in St Paul's the organ-case and choir stalls are his. He decorated many great houses, most notably Petworth, in Sussex. He sculpted the statues of Charles II at the Royal Exchange and at Chelsea Hospital, and James II's statue in front of the National Gallery.

Gibbons was a master of still-life carving; his work

George
Inn,
Southwark

was of exquisite finesse and delicacy. His preferred
subjects were fruit, flowers and lace motifs. For most
of his life he lived in Bow Street and was buried in St
Paul's, Covent Garden.

**Gipsy Moth IV**, in which Sir Francis Chichester
sailed round the world, is on view at Greenwich Pier,
alongside the *Cutty Sark*.

**Grosvenor Square**, W1, was named after Sir
Richard Grosvenor. He developed the site at the end
of the 17th century over a temporary fort which the
citizens of London had constructed to defend the city
from Charles I.

The square is now the official centre of American
London. The American Embassy, built in 1958–61,
was designed by Eero Saarinen and occupies the whole
of the west side. The public gardens in the square are

dominated by the bronze statue of Franklin D. Roosevelt.

John Adams, who succeeded George Washington as President, lived at No. 9 (one of the few old houses remaining) in 1785 when he acted as his country's ambassador. In the Grosvenor Chapel, just off the square in South Audley Street, is a tablet which commemorates the link between the American Armed Forces and the church.

The **Guards Crimea Memorial**, in Waterloo Place, SW1, carries figures of guardsmen which are cast from captured Russian cannons at the Battle of Sebastopol. The guns at the rear of the memorial were some of those actually used by the Russians.

**Guildhall**, in King Street, Cheapside, EC2, is the City of London's Hall where the Court of Common Council, which administers the City, meets. It is used for municipal meetings, the election of the Lord Mayor and Sheriffs, and for State banquets. Guildhall has always been the heart of the City and the centre of City law and administration.

The original building dates from 1411, though a hall of some kind stood on the site in the reign of Edward the Confessor. It suffered badly during the Great Fire of 1666, was rebuilt but damaged again in 1940 when the roof of the Great Hall was destroyed and the stained glass windows were broken.

Gog and Magog, two carved figures in brown-green paint picked out in gold, are over nine feet high and stand at the far end of the Great Hall in Guildhall, guarding the Musician's Gallery. The original statues were destroyed in the Great Fire of 1666, and their replacements met a similar fate during the Second World War.

Also destroyed were the Aldermen's Court Room and the Council Chamber. Restoration was made to the designs of Sir Giles Scott in 1952. The eastern

Guards
Crimea
Memorial,
Waterloo
Place

Interior of
Guildhall,

crypt, which escaped the bombing, has the finest example of medieval groined vaulting in London.

The Corporation Art Gallery houses the permanent collection of the Corporation of London, consisting chiefly of 19th-century British paintings of great State occasions.

The Guildhall Library, established in 1824, contains the First, Second and Fourth Folios of Shakespeare, a map of London of 1591 and a deed of sale for a house, signed by Shakespeare. It is the largest public general reference library in London, but its particular strength is still its unrivalled London collection.

Adjoining the Library is the Museum of the Clockmakers' Company, where there is a most interesting collection of clocks and watches.

**Hampstead Heath**, which covers more than 800 acres, is a wild, elevated, sandy heathland on the summit and northern slopes of Hampstead Hill, stretching from Parliament Hill Fields to Golders Hill. It is kept in its natural state, and contains a variety of wild life that one would hardly expect to find only four miles from the centre of London. There are facilities for all sorts of games, bathing in natural lakes or a modern lido, fishing, model yacht sailing, kite and model aeroplane flying, toboganning and skiing in winter. Fairs are held on the Heath at Bank Holidays.

**Hampton Court Palace**, Hampton Court, Middlesex, was built between 1515 and 1520 for Cardinal Wolsey who, shortly before his downfall, presented it to Henry VIII. Henry enlarged it, the additions including the Great Hall and Chapel; he also laid down the first tennis court in England. William and Mary made major alterations, though the Tudor fabric was preserved, adding Fountain Court and the garden front, which Wren designed. The gardens were laid out in a formal Dutch style.

Among the many splendid sights are the astronomical clock in the second courtyard over Anne Boleyn's Gateway, erected in 1540 and still in working order; the Great Hall with its hammer-beam roof; the Haunted Gallery; the Tudor kitchens; the Great Vine, planted in 1769; and the Maze, with hedges six feet high and two feet thick.

Hampton Court Palace is, in fact, the most beautiful royal palace in the country. Its historical associations, architecture, art treasures and landscape gardening are without parallel anywhere. Though the main buildings are open to the public, part of the palace is used for 'grace and favour' residences allotted by the Crown.

The **Haymarket Theatre**, in the Haymarket, sw1, was founded in 1720, and rebuilt by John Nash in 1821. Its elegant columned portico makes it stand out in this wide street, which was originally a market.

**Henry VIII's Wine Cellar**, Whitehall, sw1, is, with

Hampton Court: west side of Clock Court

the Banqueting House, all that remains of the Palace of
Whitehall. It is a genuine Tudor cellar built for
Cardinal Wolsey.

**Highgate Cemetery**, in Swain's Lane, Highgate,
N6, adjoining Waterlow Park, is one of the strangest
places in London, and the creepiest. Opened in 1839
and covering 20 acres, it is like something out of a
Gothic horror film, the highlight being the Egyptian-
type catacombs, a sunken rotunda lined with crumbling
stucco-faced vaults, with coffins on the ledges. In the
older part of the cemetery Michael Faraday and Mrs
Henry Wood are buried, and in the newer part Karl
Marx, Herbert Spencer and George Eliot.

**Hogarth's House**, Chiswick, W4, was the country
villa in which William Hogarth (1697–1764) lived from
1749 to his death. He is buried in the nearby churchyard of St Nicholas. The house, a typical example of
Queen Anne architecture, was opened as a museum in

1904 and contains some of Hogarth's drawings, engravings and relics.

**Horse Guards**, Whitehall, SW1, was designed by William Kent in 1750–60 and erected on the site of the old guard house of the Palace of Whitehall. It now contains government offices, but a mounted guard is still posted there daily, and two dismounted sentries stand at the other side of the archway. At 11 a.m. (10 a.m. on Sundays) the Guard on duty is changed in an interesting half-hour ceremony.

Horse Guards Parade, approached through the central archway, is the site of the tilt-yard of the old Palace, and here the ceremony of Trooping the Colour takes place on the sovereign's official birthday in June.

The **House of St Barnabas**, 1 Greek Street, W1, is an elegant Georgian house built about 1746 and now occupied by a charitable organization. The interior is magnificent with its elaborate rococo ceilings and fireplaces, a wrought-iron balustrade and delicate 'crinoline' staircase. The small paved garden has an ancient mulberry tree in it.

The **Houses of Parliament**, once known as the Palace of Westminster, was a royal residence from the time of Edward the Confessor until Henry VIII took over Whitehall Palace. In 1547 it became the permanent home of Parliament. In 1834 the old Palace was almost totally destroyed by fire, its successor being the Gothic-style building (in deference to nearby Westminster Abbey) designed by Sir Charles Barry and Augustus Pugin. This was begun in 1840 and opened in 1852. Westminster Hall, the finest Norman hall in England, which William Rufus had added to the Palace, and the crypt and cloisters of St Stephen's Chapel, which had escaped the fire of 1834, were incorporated in the new building. The Houses of Parliament cover eight acres, contain 1,100 rooms, two miles of passages and 100 staircases. The House of

Victoria Tower and Houses of Parliament

(*below*) Horse Guards from St James's Park

Commons occupies the north half and the House of Lords the south half of the building. The west front is interrupted by Westminster Hall, with its famous hammer-beam roof spanning nearly 70 feet. This hall stands between New Palace Yard and Old Palace Yard. The east front is the river façade, which is embellished with statues and the royal arms of the sovereigns from William the Conqueror to Victoria.

At the south-west corner is the Victoria Tower, completed in 1860; the Central Spire rises above the Central Hall; and the Clock Tower contains Big Ben. In 1941 the House of Commons was severely damaged by bombs, and a new chamber, designed by Sir Giles Scott, was opened in 1950. In the gardens of Victoria Tower there is a bronze group by Rodin—*The Burghers of Calais*.

When the House is in session a Union Jack flies from the Victoria Tower during the day; at night a light shines in the Clock Tower above Big Ben.

**Hyde Park Corner**, SW1, is London's busiest traffic centre, though until the beginning of the 19th century London ended here and the country began. There is a bronze statue of the Duke of Wellington on horseback facing Apsley House, and war memorials of the Royal Artillery (a stone gun by C. S. Jagger, 1928) and the Machine Gun Corp (*David*, by F. Derwent Wood, 1925). The Wellington Arch, opposite Constitution Hill, was designed by Decimus Burton in 1828. Originally it stood opposite the main entrance to Hyde Park. The sculptured frieze on the screen is based on the Elgin Marbles in the British Museum. A huge equestrian statue of Wellington once stood on top of the arch, but it was taken down when the arch was moved, and replaced by *Victory*, a bronze group by Adrian Jones.

This is a combined guild and university of the legal profession. Physically it is a complex of courts centring round great halls and chapels, with alleys, lawns, gardens and fountains in enclosed yards that stretch between the Thames and Fleet Street; and between Chancery Lane and Lincoln's Inn Fields, continuing in Gray's Inn. During the centuries the buildings have been much altered; they were savagely bombed but have been well restored. The architecture reflects predominantly a classical idiom, especially Temple Church, Lincoln's Inn Gateway, the great halls and the Jacobean gateway on Fleet Street. The older fabric which survives is 18th or 19th century, but in King's Bench Walk, Temple, there is a row of brick houses with handsome doorways which were designed by Wren in 1678.

The history of the Inns of Court begins when a community of warriors was formed outside the City walls in medieval times, the purpose of which was to wrest the Holy Land from the Saracens so that Christian pilgrims could have free access to Jerusalem. The site of the Temple became the home of the Crusaders —the Order of the Holy Sepulchre of Knights Templar. The knights allowed students to read the law within the Temple precincts, and when the crusading order was suppressed in 1312 and the property passed to the rival order—the Knights Hospitallers of St John of Jerusalem, founded in 1099—professors of the common law and their students had already established a legal community which has never left the Temple. When Henry VIII abolished the orders of chivalry in 1540, the lawyers took complete control.

Today, the Temple is an administrative area independent of the City government; the benchers of the two Inns of Court, the **Inner Temple** and the **Middle Temple**, are responsible for its government. They also share Temple Church, which is a 'royal peculiar'

King's
Bench
Walk, the
Temple

Archway
in Middle
Temple
Lane

like Westminster Abbey.

The Society of the Middle Temple adopted the badge of the Knights Templar—a paschal lamb holding the banner of innocence, set in a red cross on a white nimbus ground. The Inner Temple chose the pegasus. Many of the Temple buildings can be identified by one or the other badge over a doorway or on a rain-water head. The gateway to the Middle Temple in Fleet Street has a façade designed by Wren in 1684, replacing an earlier one.

Middle Temple Hall was opened by Queen Elizabeth I in 1576. In design it resembles Trinity College, Cambridge; its roof, spanned by double hammerbeams, is one of the finest in the world. It has been excellently restored after bombing. The elegant interior is highlighted by a richly carved screen of 1574, and the High Table, made of oak from Windsor Park, was a gift from the queen. Below the dais is another table made from timbers of the *Golden Hind*; Sir Francis Drake was a Middle Templar. It is believed that Shakespeare acted here in *Twelfth Night* on 2nd February 1602.

The Temple Church, which was severely damaged during the Second World War, has an Early English oblong chancel added *c.* 1240 to a Norman round church built in 1185. It is the most complete of the five surviving round churches in England. Effigies of Crusaders lie in full armour. The sanctuary chains which guard the altar show the banners of the two Inns, the paschal lamb and the pegasus. An interesting feature is the penitential cell in the triforium.

The Inner Temple Hall, completely destroyed in 1941, was not rebuilt until 1952. The windows are a graceful reconstruction of the Restoration period. The armorial bearings which line the hall proclaim 700 years of pageantry. The Inner Temple Treasury contains the pegasus carved by Grinling Gibbons which was rescued from the burning Hall in 1941.

**Gray's Inn**, between High Holborn and Gray's Inn Road, WC1, another of the four remaining Inns of Court, was a legal school by the end of the 14th century. The de Gray family owned the manor house on the site of which the Inn is now situated. The arms of Gray's Inn consist of a golden griffin on a black shield. The buildings were badly damaged by bombs but have been faithfully and well restored, especially the Elizabethan Great Hall, through the generosity of the American Bar Association. The fine screen was probably taken from a Spanish galleon in 1588. The plaques on the walls depict the arms of each Treasurer. One of them was Francis Bacon (1606) who had chambers in Gray's Inn for nearly 50 years and who laid out most of the grounds. His memorial statue stands in South Square, and the catalpa tree in the gardens is said to have been planted by him. The gatehouse dates from 1688.

Raymond's Buildings, Gray's Inn

**Lincoln's Inn**, in Chancery Lane, WC2, the fourth Inn of Court, is named after the Earl of Lincoln who set up a law school in Shoe Lane in the 15th century; architecturally it is one of the most interesting. The Gothic-style chapel, designed with Inigo Jones's approval, though not by him, has an open-plan crypt in which are some worn burial tombs. The stained glass windows by Bernard Van Linge were commissioned by friends of Shakespeare.

The oldest building of Lincoln's Inn is the Old Hall, built in 1490–2, though drastically restored in 1924–8. It contains Hogarth's painting, *St Paul before Felix*. The screen, once attributed to Inigo Jones, is also noteworthy. The New Hall was built in 1845. The original gatehouse of 1518, made of bricks baked in the Inn's own kiln, was replaced in 1968 by a pink replica, but fortunately the gates of 1564 still stand.

---

The **Jewel Tower**, Old Palace Yard, SW1, is the last surviving domestic building that was part of the Palace of Westminster. Built in 1365 with a moat round it, it served as a treasure house for Edward III. Until 1938 it was a testing office for weights and measures; now it contains relics of the Old Palace, which can be seen by the public.

**Keats House** (Wentworth Place) in Keats Grove, NW3, is a Regency house with a charming old-world garden. Here Keats spent two of his five creative years (1818–20), living in half the house with his friend Charles Armitage Brown (the Brawne family lived in the other half). He is supposed to have written *Ode to a Nightingale* under a mulberry tree in the garden.

The house became a memorial to the poet in 1925, when it was bought by public subscription, mainly from American admirers. The museum contains fascinating relics of the poet, including the manuscript of his last poem *Bright Star*, which he wrote on the

blank pages of his copy of Shakespeare.

**Kensington Palace**, w8, originally Nottingham House, was bought by William III in 1689, hoping that country air would relieve his asthma, and Wren was commissioned to turn it into a royal residence. The interior was altered by William Kent for George I in 1722–4. Mary II, William III, Anne and George I all died there; the last sovereign to live there was George II. Queen Victoria was born there in 1819, and lived there until her accession in 1837.

The Orangery, once attributed to Wren, is now thought more probably to be by Sir John Vanbrugh or Nicholas Hawksmoor. In 1951 the London Museum, previously housed in Lancaster House, was moved to Kensington Palace.

**Kenwood House**, Hampstead, nw3, at the north-east corner of Hampstead Heath, is a mansion, set in 24 acres of park land, that once belonged to the Earl of Mansfield, Lord Chief Justice in the reign of George III. It was designed by Robert Adam in classical style in 1767–9. The Library is one of the finest specimen's of Adam's work in existence. The late

Lord Iveagh bequeathed the house and land to the nation in 1927, together with his choice collection of paintings and furniture. The pictures include a Rembrandt self-portrait, Vermeer's *The Guitar Player* and Gainsborough's *Pink Lady*. Also represented are Romney, Raeburn, Reynolds, Van Dyck, de Jongh and Guardi.

**Kew Gardens** (officially known as the Royal Botanic Gardens), at the west end of Kew Green, were founded by Princess Augusta, mother of George III, in 1759. They were designed for Kew House, an occasional royal residence that was demolished in 1803. In 1841 the whole property was handed to the nation. The primary purpose of Kew Gardens is to serve the science of botany. About 30,000 plants are identified every year, and information and specimens are exchanged with botanists all over the world. 45,000 different trees, shrubs, herbs and flowers are cultivated. The Library contains over 50,000 books.

The Pagoda was built by Sir William Chambers in 1762 and reflects the current interest in chinoiserie. The great Palm House was designed by Decimus Burton in 1848. The Flagstaff, nearly 225 feet high,

Kenwood House, south front

near the Temperate House is the tallest in the world.

The Dutch House, or Kew Palace, a red brick building near the northern end of the Broad Walk, dates from 1631 and shows the influence of Low Country architects at that time.

Other attractions at Kew Gardens include the Herbarium, the Aroid House, several Hothouses, the Rock Garden, Alpine House, Aquatic Garden, Arboretum, four Museums and a lake. The displays of spring flowers, azaleas and rhododendrons are world famous.

**Lambeth Palace**, by Lambeth Bridge, SE1, has been the London residence of the Archbishops of Canterbury for 700 years. It was originally built in the 13th century, when the Thames was the great highway of London and it was convenient for the archbishop to have a riverside residence with its own water gate. Many additions were made in later years. In spite of restoration and bombing, however, the palace still has a medieval flavour. Morton's Tower, a red brick gatehouse, was built in 1490, and Lollards' Tower c. 1450. Under the chapel, which dates probably from 1246–60, is the crypt, the earliest part of the palace, with pillars of Purbeck marble. The Great Hall, rebuilt in 1663, has a good hammer-beam roof. This hall is now the Library, and houses about 1,500 manuscripts and books, many finely illuminated. The Guard Room has a 14th-century timber roof and contains portraits of archbishops from 1503 to the 19th century.

**Lancaster House**, in Stable Yard, beside St James's Palace, SW1, is a fine example of early Victorian architecture. It dates from 1825, when it was designed by Benjamin Wyatt for the Duke of York. When the Duke died in debt the Marquess of Stafford took possession, and the house was completed by Robert Smirke and Charles Barry in 1840. It was then named Stafford House, and remained so until 1912, when the first Lord Leverhulme presented it to the nation and renamed it Lancaster House. It became a home for the London Museum until the latter was removed to Kensington Palace.

Lancaster House was badly damaged during the Second World War, and after repair was re-opened in 1950. It is now used for Government conferences and official functions. Barry's double staircase and the ceiling paintings in the first floor gallery are noteworthy.

**Leicester Square**, joined to Piccadilly Circus by Coventry Street, was laid out in the 17th century on open land known as Leicester Fields. It was named after the second Earl of Leicester, whose mansion was built on the north side in 1631. During the 18th century a residential square was laid out. The square in its present state is the work of Albert Grant in 1874, though the buildings round it have seen many changes since then. There is a statue of Shakespeare in the centre and busts of Newton, Reynolds, Hogarth and Hunter the surgeon, former residents, at the corners.

**Lincoln's Inn Fields**, between Kingsway and Lincoln's Inn, WC2, was laid out by Inigo Jones in 1618, and was the most fashionable square in London. For a long time it was a popular resort of duellists, but today it is more noted for its plane trees and as a minor Speakers' Corner. The surrounding houses contain some fine examples of civic architecture; some on the west and north sides were built before the Commonwealth, while others are 18th or 19th-century.

The Royal College of Surgeons on the south side has a magnificent Ionic portico executed by George Dance the Younger; to the north, at No. 13, is Sir John Soane's Museum.

**Lloyd's**, in Leadenhall Street and Lime Street, EC3, is the international market for insurance and the

(*above*)
Lambeth
Palace:
main
gateway
and
Lambeth
Church

Lincoln's
Inn Fields,
with Sir
John
Soane's
Museum

world centre for marine and aviation news; reports are sent out by 1,500 agents from ports and towns all over the world. It started in Edward Lloyd's coffee shop in Tower Street in 1689, was given official status by Act of Parliament in 1871, and in 1958 moved into its new building. The Leadenhall Street building was designed by Sir Edwin Cooper in 1928.

In the underwriters' room (called 'The Room') hangs the Lutine Bell, that was salvaged from the frigate *Lutine* which sank off the Texel in 1799 with nearly half a million pounds' worth of gold on board. The cargo was insured at Lloyd's and the liability was met in full. When the Lutine bell is tolled nowadays, one stroke means bad news and two strokes, good news.

The new building in Lime Street also contains the Nelson Room, with mementoes of the admiral; the Adam Committee Room, designed by Robert Adam for the Marquess of Lansdowne at Bowood, his Wiltshire mansion; and a small museum containing Roman and medieval finds from the foundations.

The **London Silver Vaults**, Chancery Lane, wc2, were founded in 1882 as the Chancery Lane Safe Depository and did not become a trading centre until 1953. The building above the vaults was bombed during the Second World War, but has since been rebuilt. In two underground corridors beneath the new building more than 40 individual shops are accommodated. The selection of antique, contemporary and reproduction silverware is unparalleled anywhere in the world.

The **London Stone**, a battered rectangular block, is let into the wall of the new Bank of China building, erected on the site of St Swithin's Church opposite Cannon Street Station, ec4. St Swithin's was destroyed by bombing and was not rebuilt. The stone is said to be the Roman milestone that once stood in Agricola's London forum. Distances were measured from it along the Roman military roads which radiated from London in all directions.

The London Stone

**Lord's Cricket Ground**, St John's Wood, NW8. Thomas Lord, after whom the ground is named, was born in Yorkshire in 1755, moved to London and got a job with the White Conduit Club who disliked the ground they played on, and Lord undertook to find a new one. A match was played on the present ground in June, 1814, and the search was over.

Lord's is the headquarters of cricket's governing body, the Marylebone Cricket Club, membership of which is very exclusive, and also of the Middlesex County Cricket Club. The Ashes—the trophy for which England plays Australia and which consists of a charred cricket bail in an urn—repose in the Cricket Museum and Memorial Gallery behind the Members' Pavilion. At the Members' Entrance in St John's Wood Road are the Grace Gates, named after Dr W. G. Grace, one of the game's most illustrious names.

Grace Gates, Lord's Cricket Ground

**Madame Tussaud's**, Marylebone Road, NW1, the famous waxwork exhibition, was established in London by Madame Tussaud with her collection of death masks of victims of the guillotine in the French Revolution. Nowadays, in addition to effigies of famous historical, political and royal figures, sports and pop idols are represented, and other contemporary figures of fame or notoriety. The Chamber of Horrors caters for those of macabre tastes. All figures are made in the building, and the display frequently changes according to who is currently in the limelight. A noteworthy feature of the waxworks is the exact detail of the costumes.

The **Mall**, a spacious avenue with a double row of lime trees, links Buckingham Palace with Trafalgar Square, and is the chief ceremonial driveway of London. It was laid out by Sir Aston Webb in 1910, with Admiralty Arch at one end and the Victoria Memorial at the other. The Mall gets its name from the alley which Charles II had there in which pell mell (or *paille maille*), a ball game played with hoops and a mallet, was popular. In the 18th century the Mall was a fashionable promenade.

When the Queen drives down the Mall at the State Opening of Parliament, for the Trooping the Colour ceremony, or to meet distinguished visitors, it is decorated with flags and banners.

**Mansion House**, at the Bank crossing, EC2, is the official residence of the Lord Mayor of London. It was designed by George Dance the Elder and completed in 1753. A portico of six Corinthian columns supporting a sculptured pediment ornaments the front of the building. Inside there are many sumptuous rooms but the *pièce de résistance* is the Egyptian Hall, 90 feet long and 60 feet wide, which is the Lord Mayor's State Banqueting Room. It has a great cornice, on which the coved ceiling rests, supported by 16

Mansion House

tall massive Corinthian columns, eight on either side, and by eight similar half-columns at either end of the hall.

The Justice Room is one of the two magistrates' courts in the City; the other is at the Guildhall. Beneath it are 11 cells, 10 for men and one for women.

Until the present building was erected, the Lord Mayor had to carry out his mayoral duties from his home or from the premises of his Livery Company. Now the Mansion House is the scene of many national and international functions.

**Marble Arch**, at the north-east corner of Hyde Park, W1, was designed as the main gateway to Buckingham Palace. It is in the style of the Arch of Constantine in Rome. Unfortunately the splendid wrought-iron gates were too narrow for the State Coach to pass through, so the arch was set up outside the Palace in 1828, and removed to its present site in 1851. It is not purely ornamental, for inside it is a small Police Office. Until 1908 it formed an entrance to Hyde Park, but is now on an island site.

## MARKETS

**Berwick Market**, in Berwick Street, W1, leading into Wardour Street, is one of London's most colourful markets—the 'Petticoat Lane' of the West End.

**Billingsgate**, by London Bridge on Lower Thames Street, EC3, is the chief London market for fish, and stands on the site of a former quay. The market takes its name from an old gate, one of two river gates in the wall of Roman London, and was supposedly called after Belin, a legendary British king. The history of the market goes back to before the time of William the Conqueror, though until the beginning of the 18th century Billingsgate was more important for coal and corn than for fish.

Work starts about 5 a.m., and during the day about 600 tons of fish from all over the world are bought and sold. It is a noisy, busy scene; the cobbled street is slippery with water and fish scales. The porters wear curious flat 'bobbing' hats made of leather and wood, with a flap at the back to protect the neck from water. ('Bobbing' is the charge the porters make to carry the fish from wholesaler to retailer.) Each man can carry about a hundredweight of fish on his head; the hats are often handed down from father to son.

**Camden Passage**, N1, is a pleasant, predominantly Georgian paved by-way running parallel to Upper Street in Islington. It has become one of London's most colourful antique markets. It is networked with arcades, boutiques, stalls and rather grand shops, and dealers and collectors gather there mainly at weekends.

A plaque in Camden Passage commemorates the death there in 1770 of Alexander Cruden, who published the famous *Complete Concordance to the Bible*.

**Club Row**, Sclater Street, E1, is a Sunday-morning market, operating from 9 a.m. until 1.30 p.m. It deals mainly in pets and things associated with pets: food, baskets, playthings, leads and medicines. Cats, dogs, birds, rabbits, guinea-pigs and mice have been offered for sale there for more than 100 years.

**Covent Garden**, off the Strand via Southampton Street, WC2, was, in the 13th century, the convent garden belonging to the Abbey of Westminster. After the Dissolution the site was granted to the Earls of Bedford and a town house built there. When this was demolished Inigo Jones was called upon to design a 'little town', and he built the houses round a central square, and this was the first square in London. Some of the buildings on the north side of Covent Garden have been rebuilt after the style of the original colonnade.

The market started in an informal way because the centre of the square was a convenient open space for the fruit and vegetable sellers who came in from the villages around. The Earl of Bedford saw profit in this and built sheds to accommodate the vendors and their wares, and he eventually acquired market rights from Charles II. The market continued to grow and in 1830 many of the present buildings were erected.

Today Covent Garden is the largest fruit, vegetable and flower market in the country. The market is to be moved to a larger site at Nine Elms on the south side of the river, and the area is to be redeveloped.

**Leadenhall Market**, in Gracechurch Street, EC3, is over 600 years old; poultry was being sold there in 1357. During succeeding centuries wool and cloth, leather, meat, and cutlery were on sale, but gradually it developed into a great meat market. The buildings were destroyed in the Great Fire, rebuilt, and later pulled down to make way for the present buildings that were put up in 1881. The main merchants are now poulterers, though grocery and greengrocery businesses are well represented.

**Petticoat Lane**, Middlesex Street, E1, is London's most famous street market and is held on Sunday mornings. Originally it was a market for old clothes and was patronized by the poor of the neighbourhood. Now it is a general market, noisy and animated, with amazing 'bargains'. The patter of the stallholders is one of the chief attractions.

**Portobello Road**, off Westbourne Park, W11, is open all day on Saturdays. It extends from the flea market at the Ladbroke Grove end to the over-priced antiques (mainly 19th-century odds and ends) at the other, with fruit and vegetables in between.

**Smithfield** (more accurately, West Smithfield), EC1, is the location of the Central Meat Market, in buildings designed by Sir Horace Jones in the 1860s. The domed Poultry Market dates from 1963, when a new one was built to replace that destroyed by fire in 1958.

The area around the market is full of historic interest. Bartholomew Fair was held there (on the 'smooth field') from the 12th century until the middle of the 19th, when the sale of cloth and wool made the Fair the most important international one of medieval England. (Cloth Fair, a street off the north-east of Smithfield, has a well-restored early 17th-century house.) Until the middle of the 19th century Smithfield was the principal horse and live cattle market in London. Tournaments were staged and, up to the time of Henry IV, it was a place of execution. Sir William Wallace died there in 1305 and Wat Tyler in 1381; many persons were burned at Smithfield for their religious convictions. A tablet to the memory of

Wallace can be seen on the wall of St Bartholomew's Hospital, and another to the Protestant martyrs.

---

**Marlborough House**, Marlborough Gate, SW1, at the west end of Pall Mall, was designed by Wren and completed in 1710.   It was commissioned by the Duke of Marlborough for his wife Sarah.   In 1850 it became the official residence of the Prince of Wales, and was the last home of Queen Mary, wife of George V.   It is now used as a social centre for visiting members of Commonwealth governments.

Inside there are some superb wall-paintings by Louis Laguerre of the battles of Blenheim, Ramillies and Malplaquet, and a painted ceiling by Gentileschi, which was originally intended for the Queen's House at Greenwich.   Marlborough House has now little resemblance to the building Wren designed, for a third storey was added at the end of the 18th century, and an attic storey in the 19th century.

Adjoining the house is the Queen's Chapel, which Inigo Jones designed in 1627; it was the first classical church in England.

The **Monument**, at the summit of Fish Street Hill, EC4, is a fluted hollow Doric column, 202 feet high, surmounted by a platform and gilded flaming urn 42 feet high.   It was designed by Wren and Robert Hooke and was built to commemorate the Great Fire of London in 1666.   It was completed in 1677.   The height is said to be the exact distance from the shop in Pudding Lane where the fire started.   Inside, 311 steps of a spiral staircase lead to the balcony, from which there is a fine view of London.   On the high square base are three panels recording in Latin the story of the Fire and the rebuilding of London.   The fourth side has a sculptured bas-relief by Caius Gabriel Cibber of Charles II giving protection to the City.

## MUSEUMS, ART GALLERIES AND _____
## COLLECTIONS

The **Bear Gardens Museum**, Bear Gardens Alley,
Southwark, SE1, is a converted warehouse on the site
of the 16th-century Rose Playhouse.   Its permanent
collection embraces the history of the playhouses of
Elizabethan England.

The **Bethnal Green Museum**, in Cambridge Heath
Road, E2, is a branch of the Victoria and Albert
Museum that was opened in 1872.   The building itself is a museum piece and an interesting example of
iron and glass construction, following the pattern of
the old Crystal Palace.   It contains some fine decora-

tive art, but is particularly noted for its collection of Georgian and Victorian dolls and dolls' houses; the toy collection is one of the most important in the country. Also on exhibition are examples of local products such as Spitalfields silks, and prints and drawings illustrating local history.

The **British Museum** in Bloomsbury, WC1 (main entrance in Great Russell Street), is the world's largest and most important museum. It owes its beginning to Sir Robert Cotton, whose collection of State Papers was presented to the nation in 1702, and to Sir Hans Sloane, an Irish physician born in 1660, who became President of the Royal Society after Sir Isaac Newton. He was a collector of antiques, botanical specimens, gems, manuscripts and, above all, books. He offered his collections to the nation, and Parliament ran a lottery to raise funds to buy them and start a museum. It opened in a humble way in 1759, in Montagu House in Bloomsbury.

When George III's magnificent library became available, and Lord Elgin offered the friezes and statues that he had taken from the Parthenon in Athens to the Government for £35,000, expansion became urgent, and the present building was erected between 1823 and 1847. It was designed by two brothers, Robert and Sidney Smirke, the former being responsible for the porticoed south front, and the latter for the Reading Room, which was built in 1857. The King Edward VII Galleries were added in 1914.

The Museum has three main divisions: Archaeology, the Library, and the Collection of Prints and Drawings. The Natural History Department is at South Kensington, and the Ethnography Department is temporarily housed at Burlington Gardens. The Library has the right to one copy of every publication printed in this country.

Among the important and fascinating exhibits are

the Rosetta Stone, the Elgin Marbles, Egyptian mummies, the Portland Vase, the Mildenhall Treasure, the Sutton Hoo Treasure, Magna Carta, Captain Scott's Antarctica diary, Nelson's Log-book, the Assyrian cherubim, the First Folio Shakespeare, and the manuscript of *Alice's Adventures Under Ground*.

The **British Theatre Museum** is kept in a gallery adjoining Leighton House in Holland Park Road, w14. It consists of a collection of theatrical relics gathered together by the Society for Theatre Research. Such famous theatrical names as Sarah Siddons, David Garrick, Sir Henry Irving and William Macready are represented.

The **Commonwealth Institute**, in Kensington High Street, w8, at the south end of Holland Park, is an attractive new building with its blue glass and green copper-sheathed roof soaring over lawns, pools and their wildfowl. It was opened in 1962 to replace the old Imperial Institute which had stood in South Kensington as a monument celebrating Queen Victoria's Golden Jubilee in 1887. Its design is a central platform surrounded by open galleries, where each country has its own section containing models, dioramas, photographs, art, costumes and products, all subtly lit and highlighted by lifesize trees and pieces of characteristic domestic architecture.

The **Courtauld Institute Galleries**, Woburn Square, wc1, founded in 1932, belong to London University and house a dazzlingly beautiful and exciting collection of paintings. The galleries are small, intimate and friendly, with an atmosphere that breathes richness and beauty. Botticelli, Veronese, Bellini and Tintoretto are represented, and there are portraits from the Dutch and English schools. The Impressionist and Post-Impressionist paintings are magnificent, centring round a collection of Cézanne's work.

The Gambier-Parry collection includes Italian Renaissance paintings and *objets d'art* such as majolica and Venetian glass, medieval ivories and Limoges enamels.

The donors of the exhibits were Samuel Courtauld, Viscount Lee of Fareham, Roger Fry and Sir Robert Witt.

The **Courtauld Institute of Art**, 20 Portman Square, W1, a department of the University of London, was opened in 1958. It is housed in one of the finest and best preserved Adam houses in London, built by Robert Adam for the Countess of Home in 1774–7. The wall and ceiling paintings are by Antonio Zucchi and Angelica Kauffman.

The **Cuming Museum** is a part of Southwark Central Library in Walworth Road, SE17. The exhibits illustrate the history and antiquities of Southwark, including finds from Roman and medieval times, coins, London charms and superstitions. Richard Cuming, the founder, was an 18th-century collector who lived in a house now numbered 196 Walworth Road. Items of special interest in the museum are memorials of Michael Faraday, the scientist, who was born in the neighbourhood; the pump of the Marshalsea Prison, mentioned by Dickens in *Little Dorrit*; and the *Dog and Pot* shop sign from Lant Street.

The **Donaldson Collection**, part of the Museum for Historical Instruments, housed in the Royal College of Music, Prince Consort Road, SW7, contains more than 300 musical instruments of all kinds, the earliest going back to 1490; all are playable. They include Handel's spinet, Haydn's clavichord, and Rizzio's guitar.

**Fenton House**, Hampstead Grove, NW3, is a red brick mansion built in 1693. It contains the Benton-Fletcher Collection of early keyboard instruments.

Among the harpsichords is one used by Handel, and there are virginals, clavichords and spinets of the 16th–18th centuries. The instruments are in good playing condition, and are available for music students to play. The Binning Collection of Furniture and Porcelain was bequeathed to the National Trust by Lady Binning. It includes a particularly fine Meissen Italian Comedy set of figures, and there are groups by Johann Joachim Kaendler.

The **Geffrye Museum**, Kingsland Road, E2, is named after Sir Robert Geffrye, clerk of the Ironmongers' Company and Lord Mayor of London in 1685. It was built in 1715 as almshouses for widows of former members of the Company with money left by Sir Robert. The buildings were then in open country. In the early 20th century the L.C.C. bought the 14 houses, each with its garden and own front door, and converted them into a museum designed to show the development of furniture, furnishings, household bric-a-brac and domestic art generally from 1600 onwards. The exhibits are arranged in period rooms; the museum is most attractive and imaginatively run, with a special emphasis on children's interests.

The **Geological Museum**, Exhibition Road, SW7, was opened on this site in a new building in 1933. Its aim is to illustrate earth history and the general principles of geological science; the regional geology of Great Britain; and the economic geology and mineralogy of the world. Its collection of gemstones is especially noteworthy, and there is a series of dioramas illustrating scenes of outstanding geological interest.

The **Guildhall Museum**, Bassishaw High Walk, Basinghall Street, EC2, is principally an archaeological museum telling the story of the City of London from earliest times. It is housed in three well-lit exhibition rooms. *Religion in Roman London* contains many

Hayward Gallery, South Bank

Fenton House, Hampstead, from the garden

antiquities illustrating the subject, the most important being the finds from the Mithraic temple excavated on the site of Bucklersbury House. *Life in Roman London* shows some fascinating aspects of Roman London, among them a horse-powered grain mill, leather 'bikini' pants, household and cooking utensils. *London since the Saxons* has pottery from the 11th to the 18th centuries, swords and daggers, inn and trade signs, and wall marks. One of the most attractive exhibits is a model of the last State Barge made for a Lord Mayor of London.

In a fourth room in the museum office block is part of the Museum of Leathercraft; the Glovers' Company has a collection of gloves dating from Elizabethan times.

Eventually the Guildhall Museum is to be merged with the London Museum to form the Museum of London. The new building, planned to open in 1974, will be at the corner of London Wall and Aldersgate Street, and will be part of the Barbican Development.

**Ham House**, on the river near Richmond, between Petersham and Kingston, was built in 1610 for a courtier of James I. Later the Duke of Lauderdale, one of Charles II's favourites, became the owner. The present mansion is much as he left it, decorated in Baroque style, with lavish and sumptuous furnishings. It was presented to the National Trust in 1948 and is now an annexe of the Victoria and Albert Museum. Much of the original furniture and furnishings can be seen, and there are some relics of Elizabeth I. The grounds are splendid.

The **Hayward Gallery**, on the South Bank, SE1, is part of the South Bank Arts Centre, and is the home of Arts Council exhibitions. The gallery is on two levels, spacious and air-conditioned, and there are three open-air courts for sculptures.

The **Horniman Museum**, London Road, SE23,

was presented to London by F. J. Horniman, and was built in 1902 in *art nouveau* style. It is an ethnographical museum, concerned with Man—his arts, crafts and religions. There is a comprehensive collection of early tools, dance masks and totems, aquaria, and many musical instruments from all parts of the world.

The **Imperial War Museum**, Lambeth Road, SE1, stands in the Geraldine Mary Harmsworth Park, in the central part of a building that was once the Bedlam (Bethlem) Hospital for the Insane. It was designed by James Lewis in 1812, and the original dome was added by Smirke in 1844, but was replaced in 1972 after damage by fire.

This museum contains a visual record of two world wars as fought by the countries of the Commonwealth, and contains more than 5,000 works of art connected with the 1914–18 war, and others depicting events in the Second World War. Most modern masters are represented. Epstein has contributed some fine portrait bronzes. There are engines of war and the means of defence; uniforms and weapons. The photograph collection and the Library are invaluable for historians.

The **Jewish Museum**, Woburn House, Upper Woburn Place, WC1, contains relics illustrating the private and public worship of the Jews. Included in the exhibits are 13th-century Rams' Horns, a 16th-century Venetian Ark of the Law, and many scrolls.

**Leighton House**, 12 Holland Park Road, W14, was the home of Lord Leighton from 1866 until his death in 1896. The interior was to Leighton's own design (he was President of the Royal Academy), and contains much 15th- and 16th-century Persian and Saracenic tiling and carving. The finest part is the Arabian Hall with its fountain in the centre, damascene stained glass windows and a mosaic frieze by Walter Crane. There are drawings and sculptures by Leighton, pictures by Burne-Jones, pottery by William de Morgan, and a Tintoretto in the entrance hall. The British Theatre Museum has its home in Leighton House. The house and its contents were given to the Kensington Borough Council in 1926.

The **London Museum**, Kensington Palace, w8, was founded in 1911 and moved to its present home after the war. Its aim is to tell the history of London, especially its social and domestic life and manners, from prehistoric to modern times. The exhibits, admirably arranged, include costumes, furniture, glass and china. Set pieces are imaginatively done: old London Bridge, a realistically glowing Fire of London, a street of Georgian shops. In the State Apartments, now part of the Museum, are relics of Queen Victoria, including her collection of dolls, and furniture and objects from Queen Mary's collection, together with her coronation robes.

The **National Army Museum**, Royal Hospital Road, sw3, is a specially designed new building next to Chelsea's Royal Hospital. It covers the history of the British and Indian armies from the reign of Henry VIII until 1914. It contains Britain's finest collection of military paintings, uniforms, weapons, medals and other relics, plans, models and pictures of battles. There is a special section devoted to army leaders.

The **National Gallery**, Trafalgar Square, wc2, was founded in 1824 by the purchase of the John Julius Angerstein collection of paintings. The present building (1834–7) was designed by William Wilkins. E. M. Barry extended it in 1869, and further additions have been made. The collection of Old Masters goes up to *c.* 1900 and represents almost all the great figures in European art at the height of their powers. The Italian schools of the 15th and 16th

(*above*)
Queen's
House
(National
Maritime
Museum),
Greenwich

National
Gallery

centuries are particularly well represented, and so is the British school.

The **National Maritime Museum**, Romney Road, SE10, has since 1937 been centred in the Queen's House in Greenwich Park, which was built by Inigo Jones in 1616. The Queen's House is in the centre of two colonnades that were built in 1807 to link the east and west wings, and to commemorate the battle of Trafalgar. The museum houses an enormous and unique collection of records of British seafaring men and ships from Tudor times onwards. The Print Room contains several thousand prints and drawings, and the Library is invaluable to students of maritime history. The Nelson Gallery has many relics of the admiral, including the uniform he wore at Trafalgar, his Bible, grog-jug and purse. The Navigation Room tells the story of the discovery of longitude, and the Neptune Gallery demonstrates the development of the boat as a toy and tool of mankind from prehistoric times until now; the whole hall is surrounded by superb figureheads. (See also: Queen's House.)

The **National Portrait Gallery**, St Martin's Place, Trafalgar Square, WC2, adjoins the National Gallery. It was founded in 1856, but has been in its present building only since 1895. The Gallery contains over 4,000 paintings, drawings and sculptures of Britain's best-known citizens: royalty, politicians and representatives of the arts and sciences. The portraits have been chosen mainly on grounds of historical and literary significance rather than on artistic merit, but the work of such artists as Gainsborough, Reynolds, Watts, John, Holbein and Van Dyck can be seen.

The **National Postal Museum**, King Edward Street, EC1, near St Paul's, comprises one of the world's greatest philatelic collections. It contains about 350,000 stamps and many other items of interest to philatelists and students of Post Office history.

The **Natural History Museum**, in Cromwell Road, sw7, is a branch of the British Museum that was opened in 1881. It houses the world's largest and finest collection of mammals, birds, insects, reptiles and plants, and samples of the minerals and rocks of which the earth is composed. Outstanding are the Dinosaur Gallery with its fossilized skeletons of pre-historic animals, the Whale Room, the Elephant Group, the Bird Gallery (complete with dodo), the Meteorite Pavilion and the dioramas of Africa.

The **Percival David Foundation of Chinese Art**, 53 Gordon Square, wc1, is a lesser known but very rewarding little museum, with its collection of Chinese ceramics from *c.* 950 to 1750, given to London University by Sir Percival David in 1950. There is an un-rivalled assembly of the best examples of the Ch'eng-hua period, and also of Sung, Ch'ing, Yüan, Ju, Chi-Chou in cool, undramatic colours. The reference library of books on Far Eastern art and culture is excellent.

**Pollock's Toy Museum**, 1 Scala Street, w1, specializes in the toy theatres, so popular in Victorian times, which were real theatres in miniature, with plays adapted from real stage productions. The founder was Benjamin Pollock who, in 1873, took over his father-in-law's theatrical prints business in Hoxton and turned out his 'penny plain, tuppence coloured' theatres and reprints of plays. The Museum contains bygone toys, foreign dolls, old jigsaw puzzles, puppets, peepshows, and the first attempts at making moving pictures.

The **Royal Artillery Museum** is housed in the Rotunda on the west side of Woolwich Common, se18. This Nash pavilion, nearly 40 yards in diameter, was removed to Woolwich from St James's Park in 1819. In it there are guns, early rockets, muskets, rifles and arms of all kinds and periods, armour and models of ships.

The **Science Museum**, Exhibition Road, SW7, is one of the most fascinating and popular museums in the world. First established in 1856, it was formerly part of the old South Kensington Museum, which split in 1909 into the Victoria and Albert, and the Science Museums. It houses a collection of material illustrating the history and principles of science and technology in all their aspects, from the earliest times to space exploration. There are very fine models of steam engines, motor cars and aeroplanes, including a Battle of Britain Spitfire and a Hurricane. Two of the principal exhibits are 'Puffing Billy', the oldest railway engine in the world (1813), and George Stephenson's 'Rocket' (1839). The Children's Gallery is both entertaining and instructive.

**Sir John Soane's Museum**, 13 Lincoln's Inn Fields, WC2, was built in 1812 by Sir John Soane, architect of the Bank of England, who bequeathed it and its contents to the nation in 1833. In his will he stipulated that nothing should be changed by subsequent addition or rearrangement, and that admission should be free. The house is a typical sumptuous town house of the early 18th century, with a wonderful collection of paintings and classical antiquities. Hogarth's *Rake's Progress* and *Election* series are there; Canaletto, Watteau, Turner and Reynolds are represented. There are architectural books and drawings, and a sarcophagus of Pharaoh Seti I (c. 1370 BC).

The **Tate Gallery**, Millbank, SW1, was built as a result of a gift by Sir Henry Tate, the sugar magnate. Designed by Sidney R. J. Smith in neo-Classical style, it was opened by the Prince of Wales in 1897. Since then it has been enlarged three times. The Tate is, in effect, three museums. It displays British painting, modern art of all schools, and British sculpture. Turner, Blake and Constable are particularly well represented; the Turner collection alone occupies six galleries. There are excellent collections of Pre-Raphaelite, Impressionist and Post-Impressionist paintings. Among the sculptures are works by Rodin, Degas, Maillol, Epstein, Gill and Hepworth. The murals in the restaurant are by Rex Whistler. The Tate frequently presents special exhibitions of work by famous artists.

The **Victoria and Albert Museum**, Cromwell Road, SW7, is one of the world's outstanding art museums, with its collections of fine and applied arts of all countries, periods and styles. Among the special treasures are Raphael cartoons of 1516, paintings and sketches by John Constable, a collection of English miniatures, and an excellent collection of prints. There are displays of ceramics, engravings, metalwork, textiles and woodwork, costumes, arms and armour, jewellery, porcelain, clocks and musical instruments. Certain rooms are devoted to English furniture and decorative arts from 1500 to 1860.

The building was designed by Sir Aston Webb and built in 1899–1909. The central tower was modelled on the imperial crown. The façade is decorated in the Renaissance style with sculptures and figures set in niches.

The **Wallace Collection**, Hertford House, Manchester Square, W1, is a private collection of outstanding works of art that was bequeathed to the nation by Lady Wallace, widow of Sir Richard Wallace, in 1897, and was opened to the public in 1900. Hertford House was built in 1776–88 for the Duke of Manchester, and later became the home of the Marquesses of Hertford. It has been altered considerably but is still a good example of the great town houses of the period.

There are fine paintings of many schools and periods. Boucher, Watteau and Fragonard are represented; there are four Rembrandts, a Titian, some Rubens,

Canaletto and Guardi. There are also important collections of French furniture and European armour. The Sèvres porcelain is set out as it would have been in a gentleman's private residence. By the terms of the bequest nothing can be added to or taken away from the exhibits.

The **Wellcome Institute of the History of Medicine**, in Euston Road, NW1, contains a collection of many thousands of exhibits dealing with the history of medicine and its related sciences. It was founded by Sir Henry Wellcome, the owner of a pharmaceutical firm, in 1913. The Library contains manuscripts and books from the 11th to the 20th centuries. The scientific apparatus ranges from Ancient Egyptian to 19th-century, and in the entrance hall there are recreations of 17th- and 18th-century pharmacies with contemporary equipment.

The **William Morris Gallery**, Lloyd Park, Forest Road, E17, contains an interesting collection of Morris's original designs, some personal relics and examples of the craftsmanship of the Morris looms and presses. There is also the Sir Frank Brangwyn collection of paintings and sculpture.

---

**Nelson's Column** in Trafalgar Square was designed by William Railton and erected in 1840–3. It is made of Devon granite and is just over 184 feet high. The statue of Nelson at the top is 17 feet high and was sculpted by Edward Hodges Baily. (See entry: Trafalgar Square).

**New Scotland Yard**, the headquarters of London's Metropolitan Police, has occupied a modern skyscraper block in Victoria Street, SW1, since 1967. It houses the Flying Squad, the Murder Squad, the Criminal Record Office and an Information Room.

Old
Curiosity
Shop

It is the headquarters of 20,000 police officers. The first 'Yard' was in the Charing Cross area from 1829 until 1890, until a larger one was built on Victoria Embankment, near the Houses of Parliament. Part of the stone was granite quarried by Dartmoor convicts.

The **Old Curiosity Shop**, in Portsmouth Street, WC2, is quite unconnected with Dickens, in spite of its name. Built about the end of the 16th century, it is one of the few surviving Tudor houses in London, and was probably a dairy on an estate that Charles II presented to the Duchess of Portsmouth. In 1839, when *The Old Curiosity Shop* was written, the premises belonged to a sign painter; the words 'Immortalized by Charles Dickens' were not added to the shop front until 1869. It is now an antique and gift shop.

The **Old Royal Observatory** (Flamsteed House), in Greenwich Park, is now an extension of the National Maritime Museum dealing with astronomy and navigation. Flamsteed House was founded by Charles II in 1675 and designed by Wren. The Octagon Room is very much as Wren left it. John Flamsteed was the first Astronomer Royal; his bust is over the door, and many of the instruments with which he worked are on view. The zero meridian of longitude passes along the line of a path outside the house (hence Greenwich Mean Time), and a mast on the east turret carries a golden ball which falls precisely at 13.00 hours every day, by which mariners can set their chronometers.

The **Old Vic Theatre**, in Waterloo Road, SE1, was opened in 1818 as the Coburg Theatre, and for many years was the home of lurid melodramas. In 1833 it became the Royal Victoria Hall. Emma Cons acquired it in 1880 and changed its character entirely; melodrama gave way to grand opera and classical plays for the edification of the working classes. Her niece, Lilian Baylis, became manager at the end of the 19th century, and in 1914 formed her Shakespearean company. The theatre is now the temporary home of the National Theatre until a new building is completed on the South Bank.

**Pall Mall**, SW1, gets its name from the old game of *paille maille* which Charles II played in St James's Park. This street links Trafalgar Square with St James's Palace, and is the centre of London's clubland. The Athenaeum, United Services Club, Junior Carlton, Army and Navy, Travellers' Club and Reform Club are to be found there, still bearing an air of early 19th-century opulence.

**Piccadilly Circus** derives its name from 'pickadille', a type of neckware (or edging for ruffs) popular in the 18th century. The story is that a retired tailor who had made his fortune from pickadilles bought a house in what is now Great Windmill Street, and his snobbish neighbours, mocking his pretensions to gentility, called the house Pickadille Hall. Piccadilly Circus was laid out in the late 19th century, and though the buildings have changed, it still remains the heart of the entertainment world of the West End. Eros was installed in 1893. Piccadilly Circus Underground Station, a miracle of engineering in its time, was

Post Office Tower

(*below*) Piccadilly Circus and Regent Street

opened in 1928. Plans for the redevelopment of Piccadilly are constantly under review.

The **Planetarium**, adjoining Madame Tussaud's in Marylebone Road, NW1, with its green copper dome set on a concrete base, contains a £100,000 Zeiss projector weighing more than two tons. It can show the position of the stars and planets as they appear from any place on earth, at any moment in time, from 50 BC to 2,000 years into the future.

The **Post Office Tower**, Howland Street, off Tottenham Court Road, W1, is the highest building in the United Kingdom, 580 feet high, with another 40 feet of aerial. It was built to facilitate telecommunications without interference from other tall buildings. Its distinctive feature is the hollow shaft of reinforced concrete from which successive floors are cantilevered. At a height of 540 feet is a revolving restaurant which is reached by express lift, and is open to the public.

**Prince Henry's Room**, 17 Fleet Street, EC4, over the entrance to Inner Temple Lane, takes its name from the eldest son of James I, who died in 1612. Prince Henry's picture hangs over the mantelpiece and his coat of arms is in one of the window lights.

The plaster ceiling and the carved oak panelling are Jacobean.

The **Public Record Office**, in Chancery Lane, WC2, is a 19th-century building in Tudor style, which occupies the site of the Chapel of the House of the Converts, founded by Henry III for Jews who had embraced Christianity. The remains of the 13th-century chancel are affixed to a wall in the garden. The Public Record Office is the nation's principal repository for public archives, documents and state papers. In the Museum are the two volumes of the Norman Domesday Book, examples of Caxton's earliest printing, the log of Nelson's *Victory*, Wellington's despatch from Waterloo, royal signatures, an angry letter from Queen Elizabeth I, and the wills of such famous people as Shakespeare, Doctor Johnson, Handel, Nelson and William Penn. There are letters from George Washington to George III, and the 'Olive Branch Petition' to George III sent from Congress in 1775.

The **Queen's House**, Greenwich, is part of the National Maritime Museum, and is a very fine example of Inigo Jones's Palladian style. Instead of a central courtyard, an entrance hall opens on to all parts of the house, the first house in England to be so designed. It was started in 1617, but not finished until 1635, and then it was occupied by Charles I and his wife Henrietta Maria. Its chief feature is a most beautiful cantilevered staircase; the elegant iron balustrade with its 'tulip' motif winds up to the top of the house. The craftsmanship of the marble floors and the carved and painted ceilings is equally noteworthy.

## RAILWAY STATIONS ——————————

**Euston Station** was London's first main line terminus for trains running between London and Birmingham. Designed by Philip Hardwick, it was built in 1837. Hardwick's great Doric arch made an impressive approach and the Great Hall was added in 1846 with its magnificent staircase leading up to the Shareholders' Room. It became the terminus for trains from Scotland and the north of England, and from Euston the Irish Mail set off on its nightly journey to Holyhead. In the 1960s, when electricity had finally taken over from steam, the entire station was rebuilt, and today it is London's most modern station.

**King's Cross Station** was opened in 1852 and was named after a statue of George IV that used to stand near by. The station was designed by Lewis Cubitt in a style that was solid, unfussy and functional. The clock surmounting the façade came from the Great Exhibition of 1851. King's Cross serves Scotland and the north, and it is from here that *The Flying Scotsman* leaves on its journey to Edinburgh.

**Paddington Station** serves the west of England. It was designed by Isambard Kingdom Brunel and Matthew Digby Wyatt, and was opened in 1854. Before all the land was acquired a temporary terminus for the Great Western Railway was built near by, and it was at this station that Queen Victoria arrived on her first train journey from Slough in 1842.

**St Pancras Station** is King's Cross's next-door neighbour, but in style is very different. The station is entirely overshadowed by Sir Gilbert Scott's enormous Gothic-type hotel. The station itself, designed by W. H. Barlow, is roofed by a 250-foot iron span which was the world's largest at the time of its construction, and was opened in 1867. The hotel was completed ten years later. It ceased to be a hotel some years ago and is now used as offices. St Pancras serves the midlands and the north.

**Victoria Station** was opened in 1860. Its building was strongly opposed by influential local residents who feared that noise and smoke would cause them great inconvenience, but Parliament approved the plans, with the proviso that the tracks crossing the Thames should be enclosed in a steel and glass tunnel. In 1902 the station was completely rebuilt with an ornate frontage and a large forecourt.

**Waterloo Station** was opened in 1922. It was built above ground level and is probably London's best planned station. The huge concourse gives direct access to all the platforms. Waterloo has many commuter services. It also serves Southampton and the south, and receives boat trains from Southampton and Weymouth. The original station was opened in 1848,

(*above*)
St Pancras
Station

Law
Courts
(Royal
Courts of
Justice)

and as it grew busier platforms were added to cope with the extra traffic. At the turn of the century rebuilding became necessary, and the present station was eventually completed.

---

**Regent Street**, W1, is part of the processional way that John Nash planned in his attempt to link Regent's Park with Carlton House Terrace. It was built in the early part of the 19th century but has been entirely rebuilt since and has lost much of the grace and charm that old prints show it once had. The curved part of the street near Piccadilly Circus, called the Quadrant, is the only part that retains some of the spirit of the Nash composition.

The **Roman Bath**, 5 Strand Lane, WC2, is of uncertain origin; it is almost certainly not Roman, perhaps Tudor. The oval lead overflow pipe may be genuinely Roman, but the bricks are small and non-porous, and of an unusual type. Near by are the remains of an Elizabethan bath said to date from 1588. The National Trust owns the property.

The **Royal Courts of Justice** (commonly called the Law Courts), Strand, WC2, were built in 1874–82 for the Supreme Court of Judicature when it was moved from Westminster Palace. The style is Victorian monastic Gothic. Inside, the chief feature is the Central Hall, which is 238 feet long and 80 feet high. It has organ-pipe buttresses and a mosaic pavement. Underneath the balcony at the far end is a bust of Queen Victoria who opened the building in 1882. The public galleries are open when the Courts are sitting, and a 'Trial List' publishes the cases that have reached trial in one of the adjoining courtrooms.

The **Royal Exchange**, between Threadneedle Street, EC3, and Cornhill, is the third building on the site. Designed by Sir William Tite, it was completed in 1884 and opened by Queen Victoria. The credit for founding a bourse or central place of business for City merchants is given to Sir Thomas Gresham, and the Royal Exchange was useful until late in the 19th century. Since 1939 no exchange business has been carried on; the building is now occupied by commercial firms.

Inside, a glass-roofed quadrangle has a pavement of Turkey stone preserved from the original Exchange and is surrounded by frescoes illustrating incidents in London's history. In the corners are statues of Sir Thomas Gresham, Elizabeth I, Charles II, Victoria and Prince Albert. The campanile is 180 feet high and has a statue of Gresham on its east face and a gilded weather-vane, 11 feet long, of a grasshopper—the Gresham family crest.

The **Royal Festival Hall**, built for the 1951 Festival of Britain, was designed as the first part of a cultural centre that was to be eventually established on a derelict part of the South Bank. The interior is very fine and has perfect acoustics. The Queen Elizabeth Hall, the Purcell Room and the Hayward Gallery are later

Royal Festival Hall

additions to the South Bank complex. A new river frontage was completed in 1965.

The **Royal Naval College** (Greenwich Hospital), King William Walk, SE10, dominates the waterfront. It occupies the site of Greenwich Palace, built in 1423–33 by the Duke of Gloucester. During the Protectorate it fell into sad decay. The present building was planned by Charles II in a style to rival Versailles, but only the north-west wing was completed, from designs by John Webb. After 1692 Mary, wife of William III, decided to extend the palace as a hospital and retirement home for disabled sailors, and new buildings, designed by Wren, opened in 1705, though the hospital was not completely finished until 1712. In 1873 the buildings were assigned to a college for the higher education of naval officers.

The chapel, rebuilt in an ornate Greek style in 1779–90, and the Painted Hall, designed by Wren in 1703, are the two parts of the College open to the public.

The **Royal Opera Arcade**, between Pall Mall and Charles Street, SW1, is a charming little arcade by John Nash and G. S. Repton. It was the earliest in London. The atmosphere is pure Regency, made up of bow-fronted shops, glass-domed vaults and elegant lamps.

## ROYAL PARKS

**Green Park** is the smallest of the parks in central London, covering 53 acres. Charles II bought the land in 1667 to make an extension to St James's Park, and it became a separate park only when the Mall was made. In the western corner is the Wellington Arch, a monument to the Iron Duke. The Green Park contains few flowers but has extensive grassland and many trees.

**Greenwich Park** was the first of the Royal Parks

to be enclosed. As early as 1433 Henry VI allowed his uncle to enclose 200 acres to make a park here. It has tree-lined avenues, flower beds, an ornamental pond and a bird sanctuary. On a path in front of the Observatory is the meridian line, which marks the zero degree of longitude stretching due north and south, and in the park there is a metal plate which gives standard measures of length. The former Royal Observatory and the National Maritime Museum are in the park, and from them one can get remarkable views over London.

**Hyde Park** covers about 360 acres. The land was once part of the Manor of Eia, mentioned in the Domesday Book, and was the haunt of deer, bears and wild bulls. It became Crown property in 1536. Queen Elizabeth I used it as a hunting ground and for military reviews. James I opened it to the public and Charles I laid out a circular drive and racecourse. Queen Caroline, wife of George II, was responsible for the artificial lake known as the Serpentine and its continuation in Kensington Gardens, the Long Water.

Royal Naval College, Greenwich, King Charles II block

Serpentine

Rotten Row (probably a corruption of *Route du Roi*), a sandy track reserved for horse riders, runs through the park, and Speakers' Corner, famous for orators and hecklers, is at the north end of the Broad Walk.

Among Hyde Park's many features are two statues by Epstein: *Rima*, which is part of the W. H. Hudson memorial in the bird sanctuary, and *Pan*, Epstein's last work, standing at the Edinburgh Gate. Near by are the Knightsbridge Barracks, the new home of the Household Cavalry, designed by Sir Basil Spence. Between Victoria Gate and Westbourne Gate is a dogs' cemetery.

Marble Arch, once situated outside Buckingham Palace, is at the north-east corner of the park. In the south-east corner a column of screens separates Piccadilly from Knightsbridge. Near by is a huge statue that was erected in 1822 in honour of the Duke of Wellington. It was made from guns captured by the general, and is popularly supposed to be Achilles, but is really a copy of a statue of a Roman horse-tamer.

**Kensington Gardens**, covering 275 acres, started as the private grounds of Kensington Palace, which was built on the site of Nottingham House by William III. Between 1728 and 1731 Queen Caroline enlarged and beautified the gardens by adding 200 acres of Hyde Park, and Queen Victoria extended them by taking from Hyde Park the ground on which the Albert Memorial stands.

The Broad Walk, 50 feet wide, stretches from Bayswater Road in the north down to Palace Gate. West of it is a beautiful Sunken Garden and to the east the Round Pond, which is noted for model boat and yacht sailing. Sir George Frampton's statue of *Peter Pan* stands on the west bank of the Long Water. G. F. Watts's bronze equestrian figure representing *Physical Energy* is famous, and there is a statue of Queen Victoria by her daughter Princess Louise. The Flower Walk runs from the north side of the Albert Memorial to Palace Gate.

Peter Pan
Statue,
Kensington
Gardens

**Regent's Park** is roughly circular and covers over 410 acres. It was originally old Marylebone Park, fields which Henry VIII used for hunting. After being remodelled, it was opened to the public in 1838 and renamed in honour of the Prince Regent, later George IV. John Nash designed the layout, and also the terraces of houses which surround it. In the northern part of the park is the London Zoo, approached by the Broad Walk. In the Inner Circle is Queen Mary's Garden, in which one of the country's finest selections of roses is grown. At the Open Air Theatre plays, chiefly those of Shakespeare, are performed during the summer months. The artificial boating lake was created by Nash; this is also a bird sanctuary. There are numerous facilities for games, and a restaurant. The Regent's Canal runs through the northern part of the park on its way to the London Docks.

**St James's Park** is the oldest London park, covering 93 acres. Originally it was a patch of swampy ground near a leper hospital dedicated to St James, but Henry VIII had it drained, walled in and stocked with deer. St James's Palace was built on the site of the hospital, and the king and many of his successors lived there at one time or another until Queen Victoria succeeded to the throne in 1837 and Buckingham Palace became the London residence of the sovereign.

Queen Elizabeth I held fêtes, jousts, tourneys and hunting parties in the park, and James I kept a menagerie there. Charles I walked through the park on his way to the scaffold at Whitehall in 1649. Charles II had the park redesigned in the French style with formal walks, lawns and trees, and an aviary was built on what is now Birdcage Walk. He formed the Mall, made it a fashionable promenade, and had the ponds turned into the Canal, now the Lake. The park was then opened to the public, though at first only the aristocracy was allowed in.

(*above*) Regent's
Park with Nash
Terraces in
distance

Lamp-post in St
James's Park

In George IV's reign, John Nash turned the park into natural-looking woodland, and it is Nash's park that we know today. Duck Island, at the eastern end of the Lake, has a collection of ornamental ducks, geese and other waterfowl. It is a bird sanctuary and a breeding place for pelicans. At each end of the suspension bridge which spans the lake are lamp-posts in the form of bouquets of tulips.

---

**Royal Society of Arts** in John Adam Street, WC2, occupies a much restored Adam building. The Society was formed in 1754 to encourage art and trade. The hall contains six large murals, painted by James Barry, depicting the benefits of civilization.

**Sadler's Wells Theatre**, in Rosebery Avenue, EC1, is named after Mr Thomas Sadler who, in 1683, discovered a well in the grounds of his Music house from which medicinal waters could be taken for a variety of diseases. The theatre thrived and the place became a popular spa and pleasure resort. The present building dates from 1931. It incorporates parts of the old theatre where Grimaldi played in 1781–1805 and Samuel Phelps produced Shakespeare in 1844–64. Dame Lilian Baylis was responsible for its becoming a home for opera and ballet. In 1957 the ballet company became the Royal Ballet of Covent Garden, and in 1968 Sadler's Wells Opera transferred to the Coliseum Theatre. Now the theatre entertains visiting opera and ballet companies from all parts of the world.

**St Clement Danes**, Strand, WC2, is a medieval church that was rebuilt by Wren in 1680–2. The walls and James Gibbs's tower survived the bombing of 1941 and it has been restored as the official church of the R.A.F. Dr Johnson's statue stands outside the east end; this was his parish church. Opposite the west end is the Gladstone memorial, set up in 1905.

(*above*)
Sadler's
Wells
Theatre

Royal
Society of
Arts
Building,
Adelphi

**St James, Piccadilly** was Wren's only undisputed West End church, and his favourite. After severe war damage it has been well restored by Sir Albert Richardson. The nave has a great barrel vault, with transverse barrel vaults above the galleries. The interior is white and gold, and light streams through the clear glass. The front and altar-piece are by Grinling Gibbons.

**St James's Palace**, St James's Street, off Piccadilly, was named after a Norman hospital for 'leprous maidens' which was dedicated to St James-the-Less. Henry VIII demolished the hospital and built a palace on the site, of which only the fine brick gateway, the Presence Chamber, the Chapel Royal and the Guard Room remain. The palace was the London home of successive sovereigns. Its former importance is acknowledged by the fact that foreign ambassadors are still accredited to the 'Court of St James', and a new sovereign is proclaimed from the palace.

There are two Chapel Royals attached to the palace. The chapel of the original building (1532), off Ambassadors' Court, has a magnificent ceiling attributed to Holbein; the Queen's Chapel in Marlborough Gate is distinguished by the choirboys' Tudor costumes of scarlet and gold. St James's Palace is now occupied by Court officials, including the Lord Chamberlain. The public is admitted to Friary Court and its precincts, but not to the State Apartments.

**St John's Gate**, St John's Lane, EC1, built in 1504, was the gatehouse of the Priory of Clerkenwell, built by the Knights Hospitallers of St John of Jerusalem as their headquarters, and is the only monastic gateway left in London. During Wat Tyler's rebellion in 1381 many of the Priory buildings were destroyed, and rebuilt under Prior Sir Thomas Docwra between 1501 and 1527; the gateway that survives is of this period.

**St Margaret, Westminster**, which stands close to

St James's
Palace

St John's
Gate,
Clerken-
well

the north side of Westminster Abbey, is the parish church of the Houses of Parliament. The present church was built in the 16th century on the site of a much older church, traditionally founded by Edward the Confessor.

The glass for the east window is Flemish, *c.* 1500, and was made as a gift to Henry VII from Ferdinand and Isabella of Spain to commemorate the betrothal of their daughter Katherine to Henry's son Arthur.

Sir Walter Raleigh is buried in the church, and there is a brass memorial to him on the south wall of the chancel. William Caxton is buried in the churchyard and his memorial tablet is on the south-east door. Other well-known people buried either in the church or churchyard include John Skelton, Poet Laureate; Nicholas Udall, author of *Ralph Roister-Doister*, the first English comedy; and Admiral Blake.

**St Martin-in-the-Fields** has a good claim to being London's most famous church, due partly to its position in the north-east corner of Trafalgar Square, the work it does for the under-privileged, and the personality and character of some of its vicars. The present church was built by James Gibbs, a disciple of Wren, between 1721 and 1726, and is one of the finest examples of his work. The handsome Corinthian portico, over which is the Royal Arms, is reached by a broad flight of steps. The steeple is in Ionic pilaster form, and above the clock Corinthian columns are capped by the spire.

The interior is especially noteworthy for a beautifully ornamented ceiling of Italian workmanship. The bust of Gibbs at the west end of the nave is by Rysbrack; at the east end is the Roll of Honour of the Parachute Regiment.

**St Paul's Cathedral**, the cathedral church of the Diocese of London, is the City's largest and most famous church. A cathedral has stood on the site

St Martin-in-the-Fields

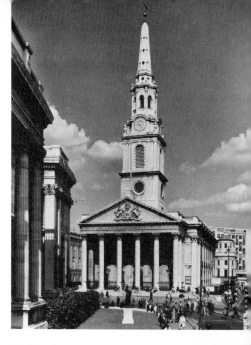

St Paul's, Covent Garden

since the 7th century. The Norman church, old St Paul's, was almost totally destroyed in the Great Fire of London, thus presenting Sir Christopher Wren with the opportunity to create his masterpiece. Work began in 1675; the last stone was placed on top of the dome by Wren's son in 1710 when Wren was 78 years old. It was Wren's peculiar genius that enabled him to combine a Gothic plan with classic Renaissance detail so successfully.

Perhaps St Paul's greatest glory is the dome, 365 feet high to the summit of the cross. Wren's technical brilliance made it possible for the lantern to be supported by a concealed cone of brick rising between the inner brick dome and the outer dome of lead-covered wood. The Whispering Gallery is within the lower dome. The exterior Stone Gallery presents a splendid view of the City. Higher still, at the base of the lantern, is the Golden Gallery. The highest point one can reach is the ball on top of the lantern—a climb involving 727 steps.

The interior of the cathedral presents the work of the finest craftsmen of the age; the choir stalls were carved by Grinling Gibbons, the iron gates by Jean Tijou, and the font by Francis Bird, who was also responsible for much of the exterior sculpture. There are many memorials to artists, musicians, writers, soldiers and men of distinction. The Trophy Room contains models and drawings by Wren.

Over the years the Portland stone of which the cathedral is built became grimy and discoloured, and a major spring-clean began in 1964. Gradually the original colour was revealed, and St Paul's could be seen almost as Londoners saw it in the early 18th century.

**St Paul's, Covent Garden**, wc2, was built by Inigo Jones in 1631-8. It was destroyed by fire in 1795 and rebuilt by Thomas Hardwick in the original style. Inigo Jones is reputed to have called the church 'the

St Paul's Cathedral, west front

St Paul's Cathedral, south transept

(*below*) Soho Square

handsomest barn in Europe' after being asked by his patron, the Earl of Bedford, to build, for the sake of economy, a church not much better than a barn.

St Paul's has always been known as the 'actors' church', and many famous theatrical and literary figures of the 17th and 18th centuries are buried there.

The **Savoy Chapel** (the Queen's Chapel of the Savoy), in Savoy Street, WC2, is all that remains of a palace that was built on land granted by Henry III to his uncle, Peter of Savoy, c. 1246. A hundred years later John of Gaunt lived there, entertaining Chaucer, Wycliffe and Froissart. It was attacked by Wat Tyler's rebels in 1381 and lay in ruins until Henry VII rebuilt it in 1505 as a hospital for poor people. Queen Elizabeth I gave favourites of the Crown the right to free quarters. In 1662 the Savoy Conference for the revision of the Prayer Book took place there.

After a destructive fire in 1864 the chapel was restored by Queen Victoria. Much of the hospital building survived up to the beginning of the 19th century, but was demolished when the approaches to Waterloo Bridge were made. The chapel ceased to be a Royal Chapel in 1925.

**Soho** is an area lying mainly to the south of Oxford Street and bounded by Regent Street on the west and Charing Cross Road on the east. It became the home of Huguenot refugees from France after 1689 and has retained its foreign flavour and cosmopolitan atmosphere. It is noted for shops selling foreign foods, and restaurants of many nationalities, especially French, Italian and Chinese. The area now extends to the north of Oxford Street, to the Charlotte Street area with its numerous foreign restaurants.

Soho Square, originally King Square, is on the site of a mansion belonging to the Duke of Monmouth, and his watchword at the battle of Sedgemoor in 1685—'So hoe!'—is, according to one theory, how the area got its name. Another is that 'So Hoe' was the cry used to call off the harriers in the fields where the members of the City Corporation hunted the hare. Some old houses survive in Broadwick Street and Meard Street, and in Greek Street and Frith Street behind the restaurant and shop frontages.

**Somerset House**, on the south side of the Strand, WC2, now houses the national archive of wills and the offices of the Registrar-General of Births, Marriages and Deaths. It was named after the Lord Protector Somerset who started to build a house on the site in 1547, though it was not finished before his execution in 1552. The house then passed into the possession of the Crown. The present Palladian-style building was designed by Sir William Chambers in 1776–86 as government offices. The east wing was added by Sir Robert Smirke in 1829–34, and this is now King's College. The west wing, by Sir James Pennethorne, was built in 1852–6. Fortunately, Chambers's original plan was followed, and the result is homogeneous. Somerset House has a spectacular river frontage, nearly 600 feet long; the great central arch was an actual water gate.

The **South Bank** is the once derelict area south of the river between Waterloo Bridge and Hungerford Bridge. Since the war it has been developed as a cultural and entertainment centre, the home of the Royal Festival Hall, the Queen Elizabeth Hall, the Purcell Room, the Hayward Gallery and the National Film Theatre. Built in unfaced concrete, the buildings are plain but functional. The National Theatre is in process of construction.

The **South Bank Lion** was once the trademark and landmark of the Lion Brewery near Hungerford Bridge. For the Festival of Britain in 1951 it was moved to the main entrance of Waterloo Station; now

Somerset House; river frontage at night

it stands outside County Hall at Westminster Bridge.
The Lion was made in 1837 of Coade stone, an artificial stone, the secret of its composition now lost, but the most long-lasting artificial stone ever invented. Coade stone came from a factory opened in Lambeth in 1769 by Eleanor Coade.

**Southwark Cathedral**, at the south end of London Bridge in Borough High Street, SE1, is a restored medieval church of great beauty and interest. There

South Bank Lion and Big Ben

are Norman remains, a splendid Early English Lady Chapel, and an altar screen built in 1520 by Chancellor Bishop Fox, who established the College of Corpus Christi at Oxford.

John Harvard, founder of Harvard University, was baptized in the church in 1608, and Harvard University restored Harvard Chapel, formerly the Chapel of St John the Evangelist. Shakespeare's younger brother Edmund is buried here.

The church became a cathedral in 1905. It is considered one of the finest Gothic buildings in London.

The **Spanish and Portuguese Synagogue**, Bevis Marks, EC3, is the oldest synagogue in use in England. Its original site was in Creechurch Lane, and it was the first synagogue to be opened after Cromwell allowed Jews to return to England in 1657. In 1700 it was rebuilt by a Quaker named Avis, who gave his fee to the congregation.

The present synagogue, unique in Britain for its date and fine state of preservation, is almost an exact copy of the one in Amsterdam from which some of the curly brass chandeliers were brought.

**Speakers' Corner**, at the Marble Arch corner of Hyde Park, is an open air debating forum where everyone can have his say (within legal limits) on any topic. Few speakers are heard seriously; barracking and repartee from the crowds turn Sunday afternoons especially into occasions of entertainment.

**Staple Inn**, in Holborn, EC1, was once a hostel belonging to the 14th-century Wool Staplers, and later one of the Inns of the Courts of Chancery. The 16th-century hall and courtyard, badly damaged in 1944, have been fully destroyed. The picturesque Tudor houses of the Holborn frontage, with black and white timber façade, date from 1586; they were heavily restored in 1937. Doctor Johnson lived in Staple Inn from 1759 to 1760.

## STATUES

Among the hundreds of statues and monuments in London there are few of men and women who achieved distinction in art or music or literature, but plenty of statesmen and soldiers. Monarchs are well represented, the earliest being **King Alfred**, whose statue stands in Trinity Square, Southwark. It is the oldest statue in London, dating possibly from 1395. Both hands are missing, but it is thought that originally they held a book and a sword, illustrating the two sides of the king's character: military and literary.

There is an equestrian statue of **Richard I** in Old Palace Yard, the work of Baron Carlo Marochetti.

Francis Bird's statue of **Henry VIII** is over a gateway of St Bartholomew's Hospital. It is contemporary with the gate, which was erected in 1702.

The statue of **Queen Elizabeth I**, over a door of St Dunstan-in-the-West, Fleet Street, came originally from Ludgate. She holds a sceptre in one hand and the orb in the other.

The statue of **Charles I** at Charing Cross was cast by Hubert Le Sueur, a Huguenot sculptor, in 1633. During the Commonwealth it was sold to a brazier named John Rivett for melting down, but although Rivett sold many objects supposedly made from the statue, it actually remained intact. At the Restoration it was set up at Charing Cross.

**Charles II** is in Soho Square, sculpted by Caius Gabriel Cibber, who made the bas-relief on the west side of the Monument. There are other statues of Charles II at Chelsea Hospital and in the courtyard of the Royal Exchange.

Grinling Gibbons's fine statue of **James II**, dressed as a Roman, now stands in Trafalgar Square in front of the National Gallery.

There is an equestrian statue of **William III** in St James's Square. William III died through falling from his horse at Hampton Court. The molehill on which the horse stumbled is clearly shown under its feet.

The statue of **Queen Anne** outside the west front of St Paul's Cathedral is a copy of Francis Bird's original work, put up in 1712. Another statue of the queen, wearing the costume of the Order of the Garter, stands in Queen Anne's Gate, Westminster. It dates from the early 18th century.

**George I** in Roman dress is one of the odder examples of London statuary, incongruously perched on the steeple of Nicholas Hawksmoor's St George's Church, Bloomsbury Way.

Also in a toga, **George II** stands in the centre of the once fashionable Golden Square, Soho. The statue was made by John van Nost and erected in 1753.

The equestrian statue of **George III**, by Matthew Cotes Wyatt, at the junction of Cockspur Street and Pall Mall East, was unveiled in 1836. In the quadrangle of Somerset House in the Strand, George III is part of a fountain group by the elder John Bacon.

Statue of
Charles I with
wreaths
commemo-
rating execu-
tion date

Robert
Burns's
statue in
Embank-
ment
Gardens;
Cleopatra's
Needle in
distance

Pan group by Epstein, Hyde Park

Rima by Epstein: a memorial to W. H. Hudson, Hyde Park

The statue of **George IV** in Trafalgar Square, riding bareback and minus stirrups, was originally intended for the Marble Arch.

The **Queen Victoria** memorial in front of Buckingham Palace is a splendid example of late Victorian elaborate sculpture. The seated figure of the queen is 13 feet high; the memorial itself is 82 feet high. She is surrounded by various symbolic groups, and over all is a gilded winged figure of *Victory*, supported by *Courage* and *Constancy*. The memorial was unveiled by George V in 1911.

The national memorial to **Edward VII** is in the centre of the southern part of Waterloo Place. It is an equestrian bronze, sculpted by Sir Bertram Mackennal and erected in 1921.

In Old Palace Yard, by the Houses of Parliament, stands a memorial to **George V**, designed jointly by Sir William Reid Dick and Sir Giles Gilbert Scott. It was unveiled by George VI in 1947 and shows the king wearing a field-marshal's uniform, with Garter robes, and holding the Sword of State.

**George VI**, by William Macmillan, is in Carlton House Terrace. It was unveiled in 1955.

Turning to commoners, **William Shakespeare** is poorly represented. The statue in Leicester Square Gardens is a copy of the Scheemakers original in Westminster Abbey. The acting profession is represented by Sir Thomas Brock's statue of **Sir Henry Irving**, the first actor to be knighted. He stands in Charing Cross Road behind the National Portrait Gallery. There is a white marble statue of the actress **Sarah Siddons** in Paddington Green, unveiled by Sir Henry Irving in 1897. Mrs Siddons is buried at the north end of St Mary's churchyard in what is now a recreation ground.

There is a fine statue of **Robert Burns** in the Embankment Gardens. It was sculpted by Sir John Steell and erected in 1884.

Another excellent piece of work is the statue of **Thomas Carlyle** in the Chelsea Embankment Gardens. A half-figure of **Dante Gabriel Rossetti** by Ford Madox Brown was erected in 1887 in the gardens in front of his house, 16 Cheyne Walk, Chelsea.

The statue of America's first President, **George Washington**, stands before the National Gallery in Trafalgar Square. It is, in fact, a copy of the marble original sculpted by Jean Antoine Houdon. Houdon went to America in 1785 to execute the work. The London copy was a gift from the State of Virginia in 1921.

Sir William Reid Dick's statue of **Franklin Delano Roosevelt**, in Grosvenor Square, was unveiled by Mrs Roosevelt in 1948 in the presence of King George VI and Queen Elizabeth.

**Rima**, by Sir Jacob Epstein, is in Hyde Park to the north of the Serpentine. The figure is a memorial to the poet and naturalist, W. H. Hudson, and represents the Spirit of Nature in his book *Green Mansions*. Another Epstein work is the group **Pan** which stands to the north of Bowater House in Knightsbridge, facing Hyde Park. This was the sculptor's last work. Much smaller, but equally fine, is the exquisite **Madonna and Child** which adorns an archway on the north side of Cavendish Square.

---

The **Stock Exchange** is one of the great financial institutions in the City, the headquarters of dealers in negotiable securities. It came into being when simple barter became inadequate to the City's needs. The first business was transacted in 18th-century coffee houses; later this took place in the Royal Exchange. The building close to the Bank of England, in Capel Court, EC2, was opened in 1802, rebuilt in 1853 and enlarged in 1885. In 1970 the Stock Exchange moved to new buildings in Old Broad Street. There is a

Temple Bar, Strand

New Stock Exchange building

gallery from which visitors can see the jobbers and brokers in action.

The **Strand** in earlier times was a riverside walk between the City of London and the Abbey and Palace of Westminster. In Stuart times members of the aristocracy built great mansions on either side with gardens extending down to the river. Among them were Essex House, Somerset House, Durham House and York House, and the names of some of them survive in street names. Today the Strand has its interesting aspects. Charing Cross Station is at its western end, with its copy of an Eleanor Cross in the forecourt; there are two churches on island sites, St Mary-le-Strand and St Clement Danes; the Savoy Theatre is known for the first productions of most of the Gilbert and Sullivan operas; on the north side are Bush House, Australia House and the Law Courts.

**Temple Bar**, opposite the Law Courts, marks the end of the Strand and the beginning of Fleet Street and the City. There has been a bar or gateway marking the City boundary for many hundreds of years. After its destruction in the Great Fire, an ornate new bar was designed by Wren and erected in 1672. The iron spikes of the gate presented the gruesome sight of the heads of executed felons and traitors that had been impaled on them. In 1878 the Temple Bar was taken down to allow the building of the new Law Courts and was later erected in Theobald's Park near Waltham Cross in Hertfordshire, where it now lies rotting in a forgotten corner. In 1880 a new memorial was erected on the site. This carries statues of Queen Victoria and the Prince of Wales, later Edward VII, and is surmounted by a dragon, or 'griffin' as it is popularly called. When the sovereign visits the City she is greeted by the Lord Mayor at Temple Bar. He hands over his Sword of State, which is immediately returned before she enters the independent City.

The **Temple of Mithras** was unearthed in 1954 when an attempt was being made to find the bed of the River Walbrook which, in Roman times, had flowed through a valley roughly corresponding to the street called Walbrook today. Mithras was a god worshipped 1,700 years ago, and whose cult was a real rival to Christianity; his temple was basilican in form, with apse, nave and side aisles separated by two groups of seven pillars.

Among the objects found on the site were a remarkably fine head of Mithras wearing the Phrygian cap of the Mithraic cult; part of a limestone figure of Cautopates, one of Mithras's two attendants; and a head of Minerva. The Temple was re-erected in nearby Queen Victoria Street, between Bucklersbury House and Temple Court. The treasures can be seen at the Guildhall Museum. In the Walbrook entrance to Bucklersbury House is a collection of replicas of the artefacts found during the excavations, and photographs.

**Tower Hill**, outside the Tower of London, was the scene of execution for traitors who had been imprisoned in the Tower. The site of the scaffold is marked by a slab in Trinity Gardens, which are dominated by Sir Edwin Lutyens's Merchant Navy memorial. Tower Gardens, on Tower Hill, are used for outdoor political meetings.

The **Tower of London** was first built by William the Conqueror for the purpose of protecting and controlling the city. Of the present buildings only the White Tower is of the Norman period, but architecture of almost all English styles can be found within the walls. The Tower has in the past been a fortress, a palace and a prison, and has housed the Royal Mint, the Public Records and the Royal Observatory. It was for centuries the arsenal for small-arms, and has always guarded the Crown Jewels. From the 14th

century until 1834 it also housed the Royal Menagerie.

The oldest and most important building is the Great Tower or Keep, called the White Tower. The Inner Ward is defended by a wall containing 13 towers; the Outer Ward is defended by a second wall, flanked by six towers on the river face and two semi-circular bastions. A moat, now dry, encircles the whole.

The Tower was occupied as a palace by all monarchs down to James I. It has also been used as the principal place of confinement for State prisoners. A stone slab indicates the site of the scaffold where many illustrious victims were executed, among them two of Henry VIII's wives. Lady Jane Grey and the Earl of Essex also died there.

Each tower has its own history. Sir Walter Raleigh spent 13 years of imprisonment in the Bloody Tower, so called because Richard III is supposed to have murdered his two nephews there. On the walls of the Salt Tower and the Beauchamp Tower prisoners have scratched messages. The Crown Jewels are on display in the Wakefield Tower. Most of the regalia dates from the Restoration in 1660, being made for the coronation of Charles II. The White Tower houses a magnificent collection of arms and armour.

Among events of tradition and pageantry that take place at the Tower are: the Ceremony of the Keys, which is enacted every night at 10 p.m., when the main gates of the Tower are locked and the keys are carried by the Chief Warder to the Queen's House to be secured for the night; Beating the Bounds, which takes place every third year at Rogation-tide, when the bounds of the Tower Liberty are beaten by choirboys of the Royal Chapel; the Installation of the Constable, every five years at a ceremony on Tower Green; and Royal Salutes, which are fired for State events.

The most famous Tower residents are probably the ravens, six of which are kept 'on the establishment' and cared for by a Yeoman Warder.

**Trafalgar Square** was designed and laid out by Sir Charles Barry between 1829 and 1841, on a site that was originally a royal mews and stables. The square was conceived as a memorial to Lord Nelson's victory in the battle of Trafalgar in 1805, and E. H. Baily's statue of Nelson, standing atop a fluted granite column nearly 185 feet high, dominates the square. The base of the column is guarded by four bronze lions designed by Landseer in 1867. The bronze reliefs on the four sides of the base were cast from captured French cannons. The fountains were designed by Sir Edwin Lutyens, but not completed until 1948. On the north side of the square Standard British Linear Measures are let into the stonework between the busts of Admirals Beatty, Cunningham and Jellicoe.

Trafalgar Square is a favourite venue for political and protest meetings and demonstrations. The hundreds of pigeons which strut around arrogantly provide one of London's main tourist attractions.

**Tyburn Tree** was a triangular gallows upon which criminals were publicly executed. Tyburn, near Marble Arch, was the site of such executions for nearly 600 years, the last taking place in 1783. The spot is now indicated by a stone slab on the traffic island at the junction of Bayswater Road and Edgware Road.

The **University of London** was founded in 1836 as an examination organization, and did not become a teaching university until 1900. It was the first British university to admit women to degrees, in 1878. Its headquarters, north of the British Museum, is dominated by the Senate House, 14 storeys high, and the Library, designed by Charles Holden in 1933.

**Victoria Embankment**, between Blackfriars Bridge and Westminster Bridge, is a broad thoroughfare, 1½ miles long, begun in 1864 and completed in 1870. Hundreds of acres of muddy land had to be reclaimed, and in doing so the flow of the Thames for navigational purposes was improved.

Most of the side away from the river is taken up by the Embankment Gardens. The Water Gate (1626), off Villiers Street near Charing Cross, marks the former position of the north bank of the river. It was built by Nicholas Stone, under the supervision of Inigo Jones, and was originally the water gate of York House. The steps leading to the wings of the Palace of Whitehall, known as Queen Mary's Steps, are adjacent to the part of the Embankment Gardens nearest to Westminster, and also show the original boundary of the river. Between Waterloo Bridge and Blackfriars Bridge the Embankment is lined by Somerset House and Temple Gardens.

Trafalgar Square

Westminster Abbey (*right*); St Margaret, Westminster (*centre*),
Houses of Parliament (*left*)

**Wesley's House and Chapel**, 47 City Road, EC1, is a late 18th-century house in which John Wesley, the founder of Methodism, lived during the last twelve years of his life. Inside can be seen his furniture and books, his bedroom and study, and the room set aside for private prayer. The Chapel is next to the house, and was first opened in 1778. After a fire it was rebuilt in 1899. A statue of Wesley, whose simple tomb is in the Chapel graveyard, stands in front of the Chapel.

Wesley's House

**Westminster Abbey** is officially the Collegiate Church of St Peter in Westminster. In the 8th century there was a Benedictine Abbey on the site which was dedicated to St Peter and called West Minster—the monastery west of the City of London. The abbey was rebuilt by Edward the Confessor and consecrated in 1065. Since then every English sovereign, with the exception of Edward V and Edward VIII, has been crowned there.

In the 13th century Henry III replaced the Norman church with one in Gothic style. The Henry VII chapel was completed in 1519 and is the finest example of Tudor Gothic architecture in the country. The twin towers at the west end were designed by Nicholas Hawksmoor in the 18th century. The north transept was remodelled in 1875–84.

The interior of the church is Early English architecture at its finest. In the Chapel of St Edward the

Confessor is the Coronation Chair, containing the Stone of Scone. This 'Stone of Destiny' is the legendary Jacob's pillow at Bethel. It was brought from Scotland by Edward I. Near by is the seven-foot long Sword and Shield of Edward III. Poets' Corner in the south transept contains the fine Gothic tomb of Chaucer. The royal tombs are in the chancel; the last king to be buried there was George II, in 1760. The Chapel of Henry VII, in which the banners of the Order of the Bath are displayed, is noted for its superb fan-vaulting.

In the Norman Undercroft is a collection of life-sized wax effigies, including those of Elizabeth I, Charles II and Lord Nelson. The Chamber of the Pyx is part of Edward the Confessor's original building and its altar is the oldest in the Abbey.

**Westminster Cathedral**, in Ashley Place at the western end of Victoria Street, sw1, is the principal

Westminster
Cathedral

Roman Catholic Church in England and the Cathedral Church of the Roman Catholic Archiepiscopal See of Westminster. Designed by J. F. Bentley in Byzantine style, it was started in 1895 and completed in 1903. The campanile is 284 feet high, and a lift takes visitors to the top. The interior walls were left deliberately bare, and the brick unpointed, so that they could be lined with marble and mosaics. The Stations of the Cross on the piers were carved in low relief by Eric Gill. There are 11 chapels, and four relic chambers in the south wall of the crypt. In the Baptistery is an altar commemorating Canadian airmen who were killed in the Second World War.

The **Zoological Gardens**, at the north end of Regent's Park, is one of the oldest zoos in the world. It covers 36 acres and houses a collection of about 6,000 mammals, birds, reptiles, fishes, amphibians and insects. It was founded by Sir Stamford Raffles and Sir Humphry Davy, and opened in 1828.

The Zoo is owned by the Zoological Society of London, a private scientific society which also runs Whipsnade, and which makes a valuable contribution to zoology, animal physiology, and medical and veterinary knowledge, as well as improving standards of animal welfare.

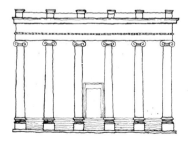

# INDEX

Entries in **bold** type indicate
text photographs

Achilles Statue, 152
Adam brothers, 36, 39
Adam, Robert, 41, **43**, 68, 113,
    **114**, 118, 129, **157**
Adams, John, 100
Adelphi, 36, **38**, 39, **157**
Adelphi Terrace, 39
Admiralty, 39
Admiralty Arch, 40, 120
Admiralty Screen, 42
Albert Bridge, 52, 54
Albert Hall, 36, **38**, 40
Albert Memorial, 36, 40, 46, *Pl 4*
Alfred, King, 16, 169
All Hallows Barking-by-the-
    Tower, 24, 27, 72
All Hallows, London Wall, 42, 72
All Souls, Langham Place, 44
American Embassy, 99
*Anchor Inn,* 50
Anne, Queen, 170
Apsley House, 36, 41, 42
ARCHITECTS, 41–8
Army and Navy Club, 142
Athenaeum Club, 42, 142
Australia House, 176

Bacon, Sir Francis, 62, 111
Bacon, John, 170
Baily, Edward Hodges, 140, 179
Baker, Sir Herbert, 50
Bank of England, 24, 46, 48, **49**
Bankside, 50
Banqueting House, 35, 44, **45**, **49**,
    50
Barbican, **23**, 37, 50, **51**, 76
Barbican Arts Centre, 51
Barlow, W. H., 146
Barnard's Inn, 34
Barry, Sir Charles, 42, 105, **106**,
    115, 116, 179, **181**
Barry, E. M., 134, **135**
Barry, James, 156
Battersea Bridge, 54

Battersea Fields, 52
Battersea Park, 52
Baylis, Lilian, 142, 156
Bear Gardens Museum, 126
Beauchamp Tower, 179
Bedlam (Bethlam) Hospital, 133
*Belfast,* H.M.S., 52
Belgravia, 36
Bellini, 128
Bentley, J. F., **183**, 184
Benton-Fletcher Collection, 129
Berwick Market, 122
Bethnal Green Museum, 126
Big Ben, 52, 107, **167**
Billingsgate, 122
Binning Collection, 130
Bird, Francis, 162, 169, 170
Birdcage Walk, 53
Blackfriars Bridge, 54, 97
Blackheath Common, 53
Blake, William, 58, 138
Bloody Tower, 178
Bloomsbury, 53
Bloomsbury Square, 53
Bond Street, 54
Boswell, James, 69, 86
Botticelli, 128
Boucher, 139
Bowater House, 174
BRIDGES, 54–6
British Association, 60
British Museum, 25, 27, 31, 33,
    36, 46, 127
British Theatre Museum, 128,
    134
Brixton Windmill, 57
Broad Walk, 152, 153
Broadcasting House, 57
Brock, Sir Thomas, 173
Brompton Oratory, 36, 57
Brown, Ford Madox, 174
Brunel, Isambard Kingdom, 88,
    146
Buckingham Gate, 53
Buckingham Palace, 44, 46, 57,
    **59**, 65, 120, 173
Bucklersbury House, 177
Bunhill Fields, 58
Bunyan, John, 58

Burlington Arcade, **59**, 60
Burlington House, 36, 60
Burne-Jones, Sir Edward, 134
Burns, Robert, **171**, 173
Burton, Decimus, 42, 107, 114
Bush House, 176

Caledonian Market Clock Tower, 60
Camden Passage, 122
Canaletto, 138, 140
Canals, 61
Canonbury Tower, 34, 61, *Pl 7*
Carlton House Terrace, 36, 44, 62, **62**, 148, 173
Carlyle, Thomas, 63, 174
Carlyle's House, 63
Carnaby Street, 63
Cavendish Square, 174
Caxton, William, 97, 144, 160
Cenotaph, 63
Central Criminal Court, 63, **64**
Centre Point, 37, *Pl 1*
Cézanne, 128
Chambers, Sir William, 36, 114, 166, **167**
Change Alley, 64
Changing the Guard, 58, 65
Chapel of St John, 29
Chapel Royal, 158
Charing Cross, 65
Charing Cross Station, 176
Charles I, 170, **171**
Charles II, 170
Charterhouse, 34, 66, **67**
Cheapside, 66
Chelsea Bridge, 52, 55
Chelsea Embankment Gardens, 174
Chelsea Old Church, 34, 68
Chelsea Royal Hospital, 35, 48, **67**, 68, 98, 170
Cheshire Cheese, 69, 98
Child's Bank, 98
Chiswick House, 36, 44, 69, **70**
Cibber, Caius Gabriel, 125, 170
Citadel, 70
CITY CHURCHES, 70–84
Clarence House, 44

Cleopatra's Needle, 84
Clerks' Well, 84
Clink Prison, 50
Club Row, 123
Cock Lane, 85
*Cock Tavern*, 98
College of Arms, 85, **87**
College of Heralds (see College of Arms)
COMMEMORATIVE PLAQUES, 86, 88
Commonwealth Institute, 128, *Pl 5*
Commonwealth Office, 36, 46
Congress House, 89
Cons, Emma, 142
Constable, John, 88, 138, 139
Cooper's Row, 22
Coram, Thomas, 73, 89
Coram's Fields, 89
Corn Exchange, 90
Cornhill, 90
Cornwall Terrace, 42
Coronation Chair, 183
Corporation Art Gallery, 102
Correggio, 41
Cotton, Sir Robert, 127
County Hall, 25, 90, **91**
Courtauld Institute Galleries, 128
Courtauld Institute of Art, 129
Covent Garden, 17, 44, 123
Covent Garden Theatre, 46, 91
Crane, Walter, 133
Cripplegate Fort, 22, 24
Crosby Hall, 34, 91
Crown Jewels, 177, 179
Cruden, Alexander, 122
Cubitt, Lewis, 145
Cuming Museum, 26, 27, 129
Cuming, Richard, 129
Custom House, 92
*Cutty Sark*, 92

*Daily Courant*, 97
Dance, George, the Younger, 42, 71, 72, 116
Dance, George, the Elder, 36, 42, 120, **121**
Davy, Sir Humphry, 184

Defoe, Daniel, 58, 63
Degas, 139
de Jongh, 114
de Morgan, William, 134
Design Centre, 92
de Worde, Wynkyn, 97
Dick, Sir William Reid, 173, 174
Dickens, Charles, 88, 92
Dickens House, 92
*Discovery*, H.M.S., 94
Domesday Book, 28, 144
Donaldson Collection, 129
Downing Street, 94
Dr Johnson's House, 94
Drury Lane Theatre, 95
Duck Island, 156
Dulwich College Picture Gallery, 46
Duke of York's Column, **95**, 96
Duke of York's Steps, 96
Dutch House, 115

Edward VII, 173
Eleanor Cross, 40, 65, 176
Elfin Oak, 96
Elgin, Lord, 127
'Eliot, George', 88, 104
Elizabeth I, 35, 169
Eltham Palace, 31
Ely Place, 96
Embankment Gardens (see Victoria Embankment Gardens)
Epstein, Sir Jacob, 89, 133, 139, 152, **172**, 174
Eros, 96, 142
Euston Station, 145

Faraday, Michael, 104, 129
Fenton House, 129, **131**
Festival of Britain, 52, 149, 166
Fitzroy Square, 42
Flamsteed, John, 141
Fleet River, 97
Fleet Street, 97
Foreign Office, 36, 46
Fox, George, 58
Fragonard, 139
Frampton, Sir George, 153
Fulham Palace, 34

Gainsborough, Thomas, 114, 136
Geffrye Museum, 130
Geological Museum, 130
Geological Society, 60
*George and Vulture*, 90
George I, 170
George II, 170
George III, 170
George IV, 173
George V, 173
George VI, 173
*George Inn*, 98, **99**
Gibbons, Grinling, 68, 72, 79, 82, 83, 98, 110, 158, 162, 170
Gibbs, James, 35, 156, 160, **161**
Gilbert, Alfred, 96
Gill, Eric, 57, 139, 184
*Gipsy Moth IV*, 99
Gog and Magog, 100
Golden Gallery, 162
Golden Square, 170
Goldsmith, Oliver, 62, 69
Gordon, Lord George, 63
Gough Square, **93**, 94
Grace Gates, 119
Grant, Albert, 116
Gray's Inn, 34, 111, **111**
Great Fire, 17, 31, 35, 37, 47, 63, 69, 70, 85, 125
Great Plague, 17, 58
Green Park, 150
Greenwich Hospital, 43, 150
Greenwich Palace, 150
Greenwich Park, 150
Gresham, Sir Thomas, 149
Grosvenor Chapel, 100
Grosvenor Square, 99, 174
Guardi, 114, 140
Guards Crimea Memorial, 100, **101**
Guildhall, 31, 36, 42, 100, **101**
Guildhall Library, 33, 34, 102
Guildhall Museum, 25, 27, 31, 130, 177
Gwyn, Nell, 68, 95

Hall, Sir Benjamin, 52
Ham House, 132
Hammersmith Bridge, 55

Hampstead Heath, 102
Hampton Court Palace, 17, 34, 35, 36, 44, 48, 102, **103**, *Pl 3*
Handel, George Frederick, 88, 90, 145
Hardwick, Philip, 145
Hardwick, Thomas, **161**, 162
Harvard, John, 168
Hawksmoor, Nicholas, 35, 43, 71, 80, **81**, 182
Haymarket Theatre, 44, 103
Hayward Gallery, **131**, 132, 149, 166
Henry VII Chapel, 31, 35, 182, 183, *Pl 2*
Henry VIII, 169
Henry VIII's Wine Cellar, 34, 103
Hepworth, Dame Barbara, 139
Highgate Cemetery, 104, **104**
Hogarth, William, 104, 116, 138
Hogarth's House, 104
Holbein, 136, 158
Holy Trinity, Marylebone Road, 46
Home Office, 36, 46
Hopton Almshouses, 50
Horniman Museum, 132
Horse Guards, 36, 44, 65, 105, **106**
Horse Guards Parade, 105
Houdon, Jean Antoine, 174
House of Commons, 107
House of Lords, 107
Houses of Parliament, 105, **106**, **181**
House of St Barnabas, 105
Hyde Park, 42, 151, **152**, **169**, **172**
Hyde Park Corner, 107

Imperial War Museum, 133
Inner Temple, 108
Inner Temple Hall, 46, 110
Inner Temple Library, 46
Inner Temple Treasury, 110
Innes, Ivor, 96
INNS OF COURT, 108–12
Irving, Sir Henry, 88, 173
Irving, Washington, 62

James II, 170
Jewel Tower, 31, 112

Jewish Museum, 133
John Augustus, 136
Johnson, Dr Samuel, 50, 69, **93**, 94, 145, 156, 168
Jones, Inigo, 35, 43, **45**, **49**, 50, 70, 112, 116, **117**, 123, 125, **135**, 136, **161**, 162, 180
Junior Carlton Club, 142

Kauffman, Angelica, 129
Keats House, 112
Keats, John, 112
Kensington Gardens, 153
Kensington Palace, 35, 36, 44, 48, 113, **113**, 153
Kent, William, 36, 44, 69, 105, **106**
Kenwood House, 36, 42, **43**, 113, **114**
Kew Gardens, 36, 114
Kew House, 114
Kew Palace, 115
King's Bench Walk, 35, 108
King's College, London, 46, 166
King's Cross Station, 145
Kneller, Sir Godfrey, 70
Knightsbridge Barracks, 152

Laguerre, Louis, 125
Lambeth Palace, 32, 115, **117**
Lancaster House, 115
Landseer, Sir Edwin, 179
Lansdowne House, 42
Law Courts (see Royal Courts of Justice)
Lawrence, Sir Thomas, 41
Leadenhall Market, 123
Leicester Square, 116
Leicester Square Gardens, 173
Leighton House, 133
Lely, Sir Peter, 70
Le Sueur, Hubert, 170, **171**
Lincoln's Inn, 112
Lincoln's Inn Fields, 116, **117**
Linnaean Society, 60
Little Venice, 61
Lloyd's, 116
Lollards' Tower, 115
London Bridge, 16, 28, 55, 56, 78

London Museum, 25, 27, 30, 33, 113, 116, 134
London Silver Vaults, 118
London Stone, 118
Long Water, 151, 153
Lord, Thomas, 119
Lord's Cricket Ground, 119
Lower Regent Street, 44
Lutine Bell, 118
Lutyens, Sir Edwin, 63, 177, 179

Mackennal, Sir Bertram, 173
Macmillan, William, 173
Madame Tussaud's, 120
*Madonna and Child*, 174
Maillol, 139
Mall, 120
Mansfield Street, 42
Mansion House, 25, 36, 42, 120, **121**
Marble Arch, 121, 152, **169**, 180
MARKETS, 122–5
Marlborough House, 35, 48, 125
Marx, Karl, 104, **104**
*Mermaid Tavern*, 66
Middle Temple, 108
Middle Temple Hall, 34, 110
Milton, John, 76
*Mitre*, 66
Monument, 125, **126**
Moore, Henry, 54
Morden College, **47**, 48
More Chapel, 34, 68
Morton's Tower, 115
Murillo, 41
Museum for Historical Instruments, 129
Museum of Leathercraft, 132
Museum of London, 52, 132
Museum of the Clockmakers' Company, 102
MUSEUMS,
ART GALLERIES AND
COLLECTIONS, 126–40

Nash, John, 36, 42, 44, **45**, 58, 62, 103, 148, 150, 154, **155**, 156
National Army Museum, 134
National Film Theatre, 166
National Gallery, 134, **135**, 174

National Maritime Museum, 136, 145, 151
National Portrait Gallery, 136
National Postal Museum, 136
National Theatre, 142, 166
Natural History Museum, 137
Nelson, Lord, 136, 140, 179, 183
Nelson's Column, 140
New Admiralty, 36, 39
New Bond Street, 54
New Scotland Yard, 140
Newgate Prison, 36, 42, 63
Nottingham House, 153

Old Admiralty, 39
Old Bailey, 24, 64, **64**
Old Bond Street, 54
Old Curiosity Shop, 34, 141
Old Palace Yard, 173
Old Royal Observatory, 35, 48, 141, 151
Old Vic Theatre, 142
Open Air Theatre, 154
Ordish, R. M., 54

Paddington Station, 146
Page, Thomas, 56
Palace of Westminster, 28, 30, 105
Pall Mall, 142
*Pan*, 152, **172**, 174
Parliament Square, *Pl 5*
*Peter Pan*, 153
Penn, William, 63, 145
Pennethorne, Sir James, 166
Pepys, Samuel, 82, 88
Percival David Foundation of Chinese Art, 137
Petticoat Lane, 124, *Pl 6*
*Physical Energy*, 153, *Pl 4*
Piccadilly Circus, 142, **143**
Pie Corner, 85
Planetarium, 144
Poets' Corner, 183
Pollock, Benjamin, 137
Pollock's Toy Museum, 137
Pool of London, 32, 34, 52
Portland Place, 44
Portobello Road, 124, *Pl 6*
Post Office Tower, **143**, 144
Prince Henry's Room, 98, 144

Public Record Office, 28, 33, 34, 144
Pudding Lane, 125
Pugin, Augustus, 42, 105, **106**
Purcell Room, 149, 166

Queen Anne's Gate, 170
Queen Elizabeth Hall, 149, 166
Queen Mary's Garden, 154
Queen Mary's Steps, 180
Queen Victoria Street, 177
Queen's Chapel of St James, 35, 44, 158
Queen's Chapel of the Savoy (see Savoy Chapel)
Queen's Gallery, 58
Queen's House, Greenwich, 35, 44, **135**, 136, 145

Raeburn, Sir Henry, 114
Raffles, Sir Stamford, 184
Rahere, 73
Railton, William, 140
RAILWAY STATIONS, 145–8
Raleigh, Sir Walter, 160, 178
Raphael, 139
Reform Club, 42, 142
Regent Street, 44, **143**, 148
Regent's Canal, 154
Regent's Park, 36, 42, 44, **45**, 148, 154, **155**, 184
Rembrandt, 114, 139
Rennie, John, 56
Repton, G. S., 150
Reynolds, Sir Joshua, 60, 114, 136, 138
Ricci, 70
Richard I, 169
Richardson, Sir Albert, 158
*Rima*, 152, **172**, 174
Ripley, Thomas, 39
Rodin, 107, 139
Roman Bath, 148
Roman Wall, 21, 22, 24
Romney, George, 114
Roosevelt, F. D., 100, 174
Rossetti, Dante Gabriel, 88, 174
Rotten Row, 152
Round Pond, 153
Royal Academy of Arts, 60

Royal Artillery Museum, 137
Royal Astronomical Society, 60
Royal Botanic Gardens (see Kew Gardens)
Royal College of Music, 129
Royal College of Surgeons, 116
Royal Courts of Justice, **147**, 148, 176
Royal Exchange, 148, 170
Royal Festival Hall, 149, **149**, 166
Royal Mews, 44, 58
Royal Mint, 46
Royal Naval College, 35, 48, 150, **151**
Royal Observatory (see Old Royal Observatory)
Royal Opera Arcade, 150
Royal Opera House (see Covent Garden Theatre)
ROYAL PARKS, 150–6
Royal Society, 60
Royal Society of Arts, 39, 156, **157**
Rubens, 41, 50, 139
Rysbrack, John Michael, 160

Sadler's Wells Theatre, 156, **157**
St Alphage, London Wall, 24
St Andrew-by-the-Wardrobe, 72
St Andrew, Holborn, 72
St Andrew Undershaft, 35, 73
St Anne, Limehouse, 43
St Bartholomew-the-Great, 28, **29**, 31, **33**, 73
St Bartholomew's Hospital, 169
St Benet, Paul's Wharf, 73
St Botolph, Aldersgate, 74
St Botolph, Aldgate, 42
St Bride, Fleet Street, 24, 27, 74, 98
St Clement Danes, 156, 176
St Dunstan-in-the-West, 35, 74, 98, 169
St Ethelburga, Bishopsgate, 31
St Etheldreda, Ely Place, 31, 96
St George, Bloomsbury, 43, 170
St Giles, Cripplegate, 46, 51, 76
St Giles, St Pancras, 46
St Helen, Bishopsgate, 31, 76
St James, Garlickhythe, 76

St James, Piccadilly, 158
St James's Palace, 17, 35, 154, 158, **159**
St James's Park, 40, 46, **106**, 154, **155**
St James's Square, 42, 170
St John's Chapel, Tower of London, 29, 177, **178**
St John's Gate, 35, 158, **159**
St John's Priory, 29
St John's Wood, 36
St Katharine Creechurch, 77
St Lawrence Jewry, 78
St Leonard, Shoreditch, 42
St Luke's Hospital, 42
St Magnus the Martyr, 78
St Margaret Lothbury, 79
St Margaret Pattens, 79
St Margaret, Westminster, 31, 35, 46, 158, **181**
St Martin, Ludgate, 79
St Martin-in-the-Fields, 35, 160, **161**
St Mary Abchurch, 79
St Mary Aldermanbury, 71
St Mary, Aldermary, 79
St Mary-at-Hill, 80
St Mary-le-Bow, 28, 80
St Mary-le-Strand, 176
St Mary Woolnoth, 35, 43, 80, **81**
St Matthew, Bethnal Green, 42
St Michael, Cornhill, 79
St Michael, Paternoster Royal, **75**, 82
St Olave, Hart Street, 82
St Pancras Station, 146
St Pancras Station Hotel, 36, 46, 146, **147**
St Paul's, Covent Garden, 44, 99, **161**, 162
St Paul's Cathedral, 16, 18, 28, 35, 43, 48, 98, 160, **163**, **164**
St Peter, Cornhill, 83, 90
St Sepulchre-without-Newgate, 83
St Stephen Walbrook, 83, *Pl 8*
St Stephen's Chapel, 31
St Swithin, London Stone, 72
St Vedast, Foster Lane, **81**, 83

Salt Tower, 179
Savoy Chapel, 35, 165
Savoy Theatre, 176
Science Museum, 138
Scott, Captain, 94
Scott, Sir George Gilbert, 40, 46, 146, **147**
Scott, Sir Giles Gilbert, 56, 100, 107, 173
Serpentine, 151, **152**, 174
Shaftesbury Memorial, 96
Shakespeare, William, 145, 173
Shaw, John, 74, **75**
Shepherd Market, *Pl 7*
Siddons, Sarah, 173
Sir John Soane's Museum, 42, 46, 116, 138
Skelton, John, 160
Sloane, Sir Hans, 68, 127
Smirke, Sir Robert, 46, 115, 127, 166
Smirke, Sidney, 46, 127
Smith, Sidney R. J., 138
Smithfield, 124
Soane, Sir John, 46, 48, 68, **117**
Society of Antiquaries, 60
Soho, **164**, 165
Soho Square, 170
Somerset House, 36, 166, **167**, 170, 180
South Bank, 166
South Bank Lion, 166 **167**
Southwark Cathedral, 30, 31, 35, 167
Spanish and Portuguese Synagogue, 168
Speakers' Corner, 152, 168, **169**
Spence, Sir Basil, 152
Staple Inn, 35, 168
STATUES, 169–74
Steell, Sir John, **171**, 173
Stock Exchange, 64, 174, **175**
Stone Gallery, 162
Stone, Nicholas, 73, 180
Storey's Gate, 53
Stow, John, 34, 73, 85
Strand, 176
*Survey of London*, 34, 85
Syon House, 36, 42

Tate Gallery, 138
Temple, 35, 48, 98, 108, **109**
Temple Bar, 35, **37**, 48, **175**, 176
Temple Church, 29, **30**, 31, 108, 110
Temple Gardens, 180
Temple of Mithras, **21**, **23**, 25, 132, 177
Thames, 15, 32, 35, 180, *Pl 1*
Theatre Royal, Drury Lane, 95
Tijou, Jean, 162
Time-Life Building, 54
Tintoretto, 128, 134
Tite, Sir William, 148
Titian, 139
Tower Bridge, **55**, 56
Tower Gardens, 177
Tower Green, 179
Tower Hill, 177
Tower of London, 16, 22, 26, 29, 34, 35, 177, **178**, *Pl 2*
Trafalgar Square, 42, 120, 140, 142, 170, 173, 179, **181**
Travellers' Club, 42, 142
Treasury, 44
Trinity Gardens, 177
Trooping the Colour, 105, 120
Turner, J. M. W., 138
Tyburn Tree, 180
Tyndale, William, 74

United Services Club, 142
University of London, 37, 54, 180

Vanbrugh, Sir John, 43
Van Dyck, 114, 136
Velasquez, 41
Vermeer, 114
Veronese, 128
Vickers Building, 37
Victoria and Albert Museum, 30, 44, 139
Victoria Embankment, 180
Victoria Embankment Gardens, **171**, 173, 180
Victoria Memorial, 120
Victoria, Queen, 173
Victoria Station, 146
Victoria Tower, **106**, 107

Wakefield Tower, 179
Walbrook, 177
Wallace Collection, 139
Washington, George, 174
Water Gate, 180
Waterloo Bridge, 56
Waterloo Place, **101**, 173
Waterloo Station, 146
Waterloo Steps, 96
Watteau, 138, 139
Watts, G. F., 136, 153
Watts, Isaac, 58
Webb, Sir Aston, 40, 73, 120, 139
Webb, John, 150
Wellcome Institute, 140
Wellington Arch, 107, 150
Wellington, Duke of, 41, 52, 107, 145, 152
Wellington Museum, 41
Wesley, John, 89, 182
Wesley, Susannah, 58
Wesley's House and Chapel, 182
Westminster Abbey, 26, 30, 36, 43, 46, **181**, 182
Westminster Bridge, 56
Westminster Cathedral, 36, 183, **183**
Westminster Hall, 30, 105, 107
Whispering Gallery, 162
Whistler, Rex, 139
Whitehall Palace, **45**, **49**, 50, 95
White Tower, 29, 178, 179, *Pl 2*
Whittington, Sir Richard, 82
Wilkins, William, 134, **135**
William III, 170
William Morris Gallery, 140
Wren, Sir Christopher, 18, 35, 43, **47**, 47–8, 50, **67**, 68, 71, 74, **75**, 78, 79, 80, **81**, 83, 95, 98, **103**, 125, 141, 150, 158, 162, **163**, **164**, 176
Wyatt, Benjamin, 41, 96, 115
Wyatt, James, 70
Wyatt, Matthew Cotes, 170
Wyatt, Matthew Digby, 146

Zoological Gardens, 154, 184
Zoological Society of London, 184
Zucchi, Antonio, 129

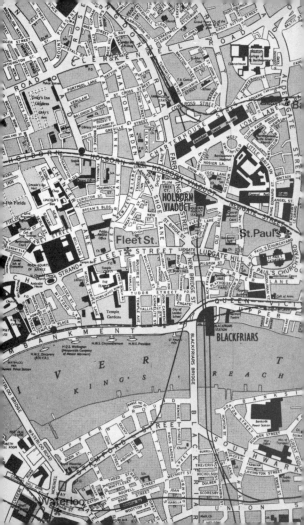